UPLOAD YOUR FAITH SERIES

3

PERFECT LOVE

THE ETERNAL GIFT

JAY R. ASHBAUCHER

innovo
PUBLISHING

Published by Innovo Publishing, LLC
www.innovopublishing.com
1-888-546-2111

innovo
PUBLISHING

Providing Full-Service Publishing Services for Christian Authors, Artists & Ministries:
Hardbacks, Paperbacks, eBooks, Audiobooks, Music, Screenplays & Curricula

PERFECT LOVE:
THE ETERNAL GIFT

Library of Congress Control Number: 2021916721
ISBN: 978-1-61314-676-7

Cover Design & Interior Layout: Innovo Publishing, LLC

Printed in the United States of America
U.S. Printing History
First Edition: 2021

CONTENTS

DEDICATION AND ACKNOWLEDGMENTS

I dedicate this book to the one who is love, God the Father, Son, and Holy Spirit. During the writing of this book, I frequently asked him to guide me, to help me know how to say something, or to give me ideas of what he wanted me to include. I prayed, *Keep me from writing anything that would discredit your word.* I would awaken during the night, and on many mornings, to write thoughts he put into my heart and mind. It's been a joint venture all the way. I trust and praise him. He is faithful.

I dedicate this book to my wife. She has gifted me with much alone time to work in my office, and she was always willing to read something and give me an opinion, a suggestion, or help with errors. She is one of my best role models of God's love, for she is always thinking of others, praying with them, and sacrificing whatever it takes in time, money, or goods, to give them what they need.

I acknowledge my brother who helped me with his loving encouragement and especially with the help I needed to solve technical problems concerning my computer, internet connections, or printer. I also valued information he shared with me on questions I had about the book and publication issues.

I will always acknowledge my men's group from Montana. As it should be in all church small groups, we grew as one in Christ's love. They were there with ideas and encouragement when I began this project of writing a series of three books on Hope, Faith, and Love. More than that, though I have now moved away, these men have been a big part of my life's support system and helping me grow in my walk with Jesus.

Of course, I appreciate the quality input and help I received from all those at Innovo Publishing who put this series of books together for me. They are more than a business to me; they do all in love.

To all, I say, "Thank you!"

PREFACE

Two experiences in my life caused me to question love in general. When I decided to ask the woman I was dating to marry me, I knew I liked being with her all the time, and I liked how I felt when with her, but was that love? When we got married, I wasn't sure I knew what love was. Having some rough times in our marriage convinced me I was right. I didn't know how to love. I had to learn. Years after our marriage, I asked my wife, "When we got married, did we love each other?" She said, "We loved each other as best we knew how." Now married over fifty-two years to her, I've learned a lot—not only from her but also from realizing that I needed divine help. I don't think we ever can stop learning and improving.

The second time I questioned the meaning of love was in a church where I had become the pastor. I was young, just starting out in ministry there, and I presented a sermon about love. Afterward, I received criticism from a retired pastor in the congregation who came up to me and said, "You don't know anything about love." That thought haunted me for a long time. I wanted to know what love was, I wanted to experience it, and I wanted to be able to genuinely love others.

Many men and women are noticing the world we live in today is changing. A lot of this change has to do with the worldwide pandemic of 2019–21 and its ongoing effects. Many activities, businesses, and entertainments stopped, and people felt isolated. The term *social distancing* came into being and meant people had to separate themselves from each other. This negatively affected the physical and mental health of many. I heard people say, "We need to get back to normal." For many reasons, the world needs love now more than ever. Without love, people and the world cannot exist in a peaceful, happy state. Without love, we do not have the relationships we need to remain mentally healthy.

In America, one of the things revealed more than ever was how divided it is as a nation. Love is what brings people together. Maybe you feel like I do that the love we need must come not from ourselves but from a superhuman source. I call that source *God*, and the God I am talking about claims to be able to help us because he says that he is love. This book is about the love we need to survive problems in our personal lives and in the world as a whole. But can we get there without the God I am talking about? This book addresses that question as well as guides us into how love is best lived out in all areas of our lives.

There is something about God that most people in the world do not know, including many Christians. We don't know how good and loving God really is. There are a few reasons people don't know this about God. One reason is because they believe in some other god, or no god at all. Reason two is that, even if people have heard of the God I am talking about, for one reason or another, they have chosen not to believe in him. A third reason is that we live in an evil world, and when bad things happen to us, it's easy to question, doubt, or blame God rather than believe he is loving and good. And fourth, since a natural human tendency is to focus on people's faults and wrongs, we don't think about God as being good and loving to bad or evil people. Who is the God I am referring to? He is the eternally existing Father of Christ Jesus, and in fact, Jesus is also that God. Jesus, who is the exact representation of God's nature, said that God loves and does good to all people, both the good and the evil, and Jesus demonstrated that fact.

People who are familiar with the part of the Bible that was written before Jesus was born see God as mean, angry, and vengeful—a God who judges and kills people. In their mind, they cannot see how a God of wrath can be a God of love; to them the two things do not go together. Therefore, I have chosen to give an example of how the God of that ancient part of the Bible loves wicked people and does not want them to die. Consider an evil king of Babylon named Nebuchadnezzar. Have you ever realized how good and loving God was to him? God gave him a position of power above all the nations of the world. God gave him victory over the Israelites when he destroyed their city and took the people into captivity. God blessed him with a kingdom of security, beauty, and great wealth.

However, he abused the good life God gave him with his partying, drinking, and using women for his pleasure. He was prideful, ungrateful, and arrogant, and he allowed the wickedness in his heart to wrong his people. If they did not do what he wanted, he would get angry and order them killed. He did not really care about people's welfare but used them for his own gain. As worshiper of lesser gods, he did not know the God who loved him and was responsible for the good in his life. He did not know that in his ignorance, he was actually rejecting the God who loved him. To be a better person and king, he needed to overcome the destructive evils in his life and become filled with the goodness and love of God.

One day God gave him a dream that troubled him. His wisest men could not tell him his dream and interpret it for him. He was about to have them killed when God helped an Israelite named Daniel reveal to him the dream and its meaning. Daniel made sure the king knew it was God who did this and not any human. Thus the king actually admitted that this God was a God of gods and Lord of kings. This first introduction to God helped him know *about* God, but he did not yet *know him*. He did not change his ways but made a huge gold statue of himself and demanded that everyone bow down and worship him or be killed. Israelites, who refused to bow, told the king their God could save them, but if not, they would still not bow. The king, in anger, had them thrown into a fiery furnace. God did a miracle, and they were not burned by the fire. The king ordered them out, and he blessed God, saying there was no other god who could do such a thing, and he ordered his people never to say anything against this God—but still, he was unchanged.

God then gave him another dream to warn him that if he did not change, he would be relieved of his position as king for a lengthy period of years and live as an animal in the field. Daniel told the king to acknowledge God as the Most High ruler over mankind and to break away from his sins and iniquities by doing what is right and by showing mercy to the poor. He neglected God's warning, and a year later, he looked out over a magnificent Babylon and boasted that he was the one who built it all. At that point, God drove him away from human interaction to live as a beast in the field. In the end, he submitted to God, praising and honoring him as the King in heaven, acknowledging that all his works are true and his ways are just and that he is able to humble those who walk in pride. God then restored him as king over Babylon and blessed his life with surpassing greatness.

I wonder how many who've read this account in Daniel 1-4 saw all the good God did in Nebuchadnezzar's life and were impressed with a patient God who does not want anyone to perish but for all to repent and have newness of life?

Now, nearing the end of my life, I thank God for giving me an opportunity to write about his love. I am still a learner but have learned much. I want to help others grow in their knowledge about God and his love so as to gain from God a broader perspective of what love is and how to do it. I want to motivate persons to seek a love that enhances their relationships with family, friends, and the world they live in. I want to help persons grow in their understanding of the God of love so they can see who God is and how much he loves them. I want to present a counter-worldview to the idea that God is mean, is unloving, does not care about us, and is not worth believing in or worshiping. I want to let people know the plans God has for this world so that they are not making a decision to disbelieve because of misinformation. I want to encourage Christians to live out their faith of doing good by increasing in their love for God, self, and others. I want to help those who feel unloved and unwanted to know that they are persons of great worth and that God loves them and desires to have a loving relationship with them.

Imagine the Creator of the universe speaking to you through his Word. Imagine listening and thinking about what he is saying to you, taking it in with a desire to understand it and have it applied to you. Imagine knowing that God loves you and is pleased with you and that he sees your heart of love and respect for him. Imagine having a new family of godly people who you can trust, who are enjoying life with you in the good times, and who are helping you get through the bad times. Imagine the day to come, after death, when your body is risen to walk and talk with the Lord in his kingdom of love and righteousness. Imagine being free from all evil and enjoying the beauty of a new earth and a world of joy and laughter with fellow believers and loved ones. Imagine that all the purest desires of your heart are realized and you are now at peace and filled with joy, more than you ever could have thought possible. Imagine that you are deeply grateful to the Lord for his mercy and love and that you are happy to be living in his kingdom, knowing that your life of meaningful, satisfying, and productive living will never end. The love you have with all others and with Jesus is deep and abiding. It is the kind of life you've always wanted, but you never knew what it was.

Now, you are home!

INTRODUCTION

In America, as in the rest of the world, we live in difficult days. According to the Bible, as a physical Second Coming of Jesus to earth gets nearer, the world will fall further away from God, and affliction for followers of Jesus will increase. Not to worry or fear, for the Lord is with his people, and his plan to save and redeem his world will happen. Since others need to be drawn to our Lord Jesus, believers have a great opportunity in these days to let Christ's light shine through them by living and loving as he taught. This book, along with the other two in this series—a book on *Hope* and the other on *Faith*—will be helpful in growing us and getting us through. Love is definitely the answer to peace and the problems of our lives and world. The following will give readers an idea of what each chapter offers. My prayer is that this book helps readers to learn more about the God of love, get a deeper view and appreciation of love, and to practice it as it is presented in God's Word. Without love, there is no lasting peace for people or the world.

In the first chapter of this book, I wrestle with the question, *What is love?* I share an ultimate conclusion of what love is, what it means to be loved, where love comes from, and how to love. The goal is to encourage readers to better love family, friends, fellow believers, and the people of our community and world. Everyone needs to love and be loved.

The second chapter points out the value of being loved. It contrasts human love versus God's love and makes a case for choosing God's path to love. To be loved by God, and to experience the ways Jesus loves us, is what gives us the ability to overcome life's problems.

Chapter three is an attempt to help believers and unbelievers better understand God. Faulty views of who he is causes many to reject God as a source of help. I discuss five problems that hinder our faith in God, including his anger and the problem of evil. God is love, and we need to see how prevalent that is throughout the Bible, not just in the New Testament days of Jesus.

Chapter four, titled "Love and War," addresses how a God of love could be engaged in so much war. The entire Bible deals with good versus evil, and God is a warrior who fights to achieve his good purposes. Surprisingly, there is a difference between holy wars and God's wars. The chapter deals with four historical periods: the conquest of Canaan, the period of the judges, the era of kings and prophets, and the times of Jesus. God's wars are to be fought differently in these days of Christ Jesus.

Chapter five deals with love in the church. Many churches experience problems because differences between people make it hard to get along. God's design for the church and how people need to resolve their differences needs to be understood.

Forgiveness is the subject of chapter six. Readers will learn why forgiveness is needed, what to know about the God who forgives, the value of judging others, and how to forgive. I also share stories of what I learned from my own forgiveness experiences.

Chapter seven tells how the cross that Jesus died on is the greatest act of love set forth by God to heal individuals, families, and the world. The reader will learn why the cross was necessary and how it is instrumental in changing and saving the lives of all who believe.

Chapter eight explains God's providential acts of love. This is one way we recognize the reality of God in our daily lives. The goodness of God to all people is highlighted as evidence that he is with us.

Chapter nine is on love and money because the Bible connects the two. God's Word instructs us about proper attitudes toward money and how love motivates us to use our money. Riches are OK, but the problem becomes the love of money and its misuse.

Chapter ten is all about what it means to love God. Referring to Jesus as a model, seven ways to love God are presented.

I had planned to stop at ten chapters, but I felt an urging from God to add a postscript on how to live a successful Christian life. Personally, I need to be more consistent in my walk with God, and one way to do this is to learn to walk by the Holy Spirit. Thinking that there may be other Christians like me who also want to be more consistent in their walk with God, I share my plan that people are welcome to adopt. However, realizing we are all different, there may be a better plan that works for you.

There is a study guide at the back of the book to help those, either individually or with a group, who would like to think more deeply about the book's concepts and consider the scripture references.

CHAPTER 1

WHAT IS LOVE?

As I shared in the Preface, when my wife and I married, I wasn't sure what love was. But there is something in humans that naturally tells us there is such a thing as love. It seems people everywhere have an inborn desire and need to love and to be loved. When we see conflicts between persons and nations, we sense that what the world needs is love. Whatever love is, we believe it will bring people together in peace and harmony, uniting us as one. We know love exists because we feel it, we find ourselves wanting to experience it, and we often feel the pain of not loving others as we should. Many want love but don't know how to get it. For some reason, love often escapes us. We know there is something called love, but what is love?

In counseling couples with relationship problems, I've learned how some define love. For example, one wants out of the relationship while the other claims to love the one who wants out and doesn't want to lose them. When I ask, "What is love?" they struggle to answer and are at a loss for words. The one who wants to leave does so because the other no longer fulfills their wants or needs, and they don't feel love for them like they used to. On the other side, the person who claims to love does not want them to leave because they can't bear to lose what that person gives them. The one leaving says the other has a problem and will not change, so I want out. The one who doesn't want to lose them attaches some sort of benefit they are getting. Of course, neither person is likely to admit that their love is self-centered or that their definition of love is lacking. Clearly, love for them can only exist so long as certain conditions are met, and if those conditions change, love fails them. Given their situation and their limited views of love, their relationship cannot work. What is love?

How can anyone answer this question? One's head swirls in confusion with the countless varied opinions and psychological studies that are written about what love is and what love is not. Besides human studies on the subject, religious people also have sources to help them understand it. For example, if persons read the Bible, they will find many statements telling them to love. The Bible tells them to pursue love (1 Corinthians 14:1). It tells them that God is love, and it tells them to love God with all their heart, soul, and mind, and to love their neighbor as themselves (Matthew 22:37-39). It tells them to love one another (Romans 13:8). It tells them to love their enemies (Matthew 5:44). It tells them all that they do is to be done in love (1 Corinthians 16:14). Even though it says those things, the question remains, *What is love, and how can I do it successfully?*

Love is like our universe—it is so infinite, limitless, endless, measureless, and vast, that one could never learn all there is to know about it and be able to comprehend it. Furthermore, love is wrapped in mystery. So why tackle the subject? I do so because I believe there are certain absolute things about love that can be known and trusted—truths that can bring it down to something we can understand and effectively practice in our daily living.

DIFFERING DEFINITIONS OF LOVE

For many people, love is about feelings. They define love as a warm sort of feeling; a feeling of romantic closeness to someone; a mysterious feeling of being attracted to someone, of wanting to be with that person, and wanting to know that person. This feeling is one of happiness and excitement. They think about that person all the time. Often, whether soon or later, there is an inner urge that enters into the relationship, one that leads toward physical expressions of closeness. Persons involved interpret these feelings and physical expressions as being in love. Love does include feelings and its physical aspects, but is love more than a romantic and affectionate feeling of being drawn to someone, wanting to be with them, and wanting to experience physical intimacy?

Others define love by what they like. They say, "I love that car," or "I love those clothes," or "I love that person." What they generally mean is that they like those things or persons because they look good and appeal to their tastes, or they like them because those objects or persons satisfy something they need or want. There is a *because* attached as the reason for their love. If that reason proves not to be satisfying or is no longer the same, do we stop loving what we used to like and go on to something or someone else? When likes about another person change, does love quit on people, and if so, is it sometimes OK to quit?

Another way people define love is to equate love with tolerance. Tolerance used to be defined as disagreeing with or not liking a person, but putting up with them, overlooking their faults, and thinking the best of them. A more recent definition of tolerance is to have an unconditional acceptance of another without any form of judgment or criticism about their beliefs, lifestyle, or behaviors. Not to accept something about another is judgmental and not loving. This definition of love is to have an unconditional acceptance of others just as they are. Can people really tolerate everything? Should love always be tolerant, or can love be intolerant? Is love unconditional, or is love also conditional?

Here are some pretty good definitions of love that you may have heard or experienced. Love is what enables two or more persons to experience oneness at the very core of their being. Love does not lock people out; instead, love makes room in the heart for one another. Love values people, placing their importance above all material objects. Love grows from a mysterious attraction into a friendship and even beyond. When knowing another is embraced with love, and being known by another is embraced with love, there is acceptance and trust. Love erases loneliness, for in being loved, no one feels alone or is alone. Love from another never allows anything to happen to us that is not for our well-being and good. To love and be loved is the safest place in the world, for in its presence and care, nothing can destroy us. Being loved creates within us a sense of safety, peace, and joy. Love, when it is truly love, will not give up when things get hard but will fight for the good it promises. You can undoubtedly add to this list many of your own ways of defining love.

Consider these quotes by three well-known people who put forth their definitions of love: (1) Elizabeth Gilbert said, "People think a soul mate is your perfect fit, and that's what everyone wants. But a true soul mate is a mirror, the person who shows you everything that is holding you back, the person who brings you to your own attention so you can change your life. A true soul mate is probably the most important person you'll ever meet, because they tear down your walls and smack you awake."[1] This definition of love involves learning the truth about yourself so you can become a better person. (2) Mandy Hale agrees, "If it's not making you better, it isn't love. True love makes you more of who you are, not less."[2] (3) When I asked my wife what love was, she said, "Love is a deep desire to do what is best for people. Love is to serve others for their betterment." My wife may not be well-known to you, but she is to me, and she does make people better, including me.

What is love? It is certainly something everyone wants or needs. When people see the hatred, violence, disunity, and lack of peace in the world around them, they most certainly would agree that love is needed to make the world a good and better place. I think most of us would like to experience a deeper and more gratifying kind of love. I remember a song that was often sung on the radio after it first came out in 1965. The refrain said, "What the world needs now, is love sweet love; it's the only thing there's just too little of; no, not just for some, but for everyone."[3]

---

1. Gilbert quote: www.azquotes.com/author/5518-elizabeth_gilbert/tag/soul-mate
2. Hale quote: www.womenworking.com/meme/true-love-makes
3. "What the World Needs Now Is Love," written by Hal David and Burt Bacharach, sung by Jackie DeShannon, 1965.

WHERE DOES LOVE COME FROM?

If love is an innate feeling, desire, and need, how did it get there? There are two primary sources of love—one is human, the other divine. It is important to know where love comes from because the source of our love will determine how we define it, experience it, and practice it. Some think love is learned through an evolutionary process of human education and experience. It is thought that love evolved in humans through their social interactions. They learned the things that make relationships work by experiencing what kinds of behaviors feel good and lead to good relationships and what kinds of behaviors feel bad and lead to bad relationships. While some believe love is of human origin, others believe love has been implanted within us by a divine source, the God who sent Jesus Christ into the world to redeem us, heal us, and enable us to overcome the things that destroy love. If love originated with humans, humans are the ones to define what it is and how to do it. If a Creator God put his love into us, it would certainly be wise to learn from him what love is and how it works.

IF HUMANS ARE THE SOURCE OF LOVE

If we choose to believe that love comes strictly from humans alone, we have much evolving to do because we are greatly limited in our ability to give, receive, and experience love. We are limited because, even though we've learned from many sociological studies what love ought to be like, all sorts of obstacles prevent us from reaching it. This is because we are all damaged and messed up in ways that hinder or block the flow of love. Our countless problems make a love-filled life and world almost, if not completely, impossible to achieve.

What are those things that hinder and prevent the kind of love we want and need? Naming a few will suffice to show why our world is the way it is. Self-centeredness hinders love. Child and spouse abuse, including sexual abuse and accompanying psychological problems, hinders love. Racism hinders love. Wars hinder love. Abandonment by people we love and those who are supposed to love us hinders

19

love. Being told by people around us that we are no good hinders love. Believing that we are no good hinders love. Feelings of guilt hinder love. Anger and rage hinders love. Resentment toward those who wrong us hinders love. Addictions like alcoholism and sexual obsessions hinder love. Fear of making commitments lest we let people down hinders love. Fear of being hurt again and not wanting to suffer the pain hinders love. Hurtful words like name calling or gossip hinder love. Jealousy hinders love. Differences in core beliefs and ideologies hinder love. Not having a loving role model hinders love. Horrific post-traumatic stress disorders hinder love. Offensive habits and personalities hinder love. Anxieties, depression, and hopelessness hinder love. On and on we could go. No wonder love is so difficult to achieve and sustain when humanity with its imperfections is our only source and resource for love.

This is not to say humans cannot overcome many of these things and achieve a somewhat satisfying and happy, love-filled life. Humans are amazingly resilient and resourceful. We are smart enough to figure things out. Psychological and sociological surveys and studies have done a very good job of accurately defining human relationships and what makes them work and not work. Many people find the help they need through counseling. Some are fortunate to have been raised in loving homes. We find many good and loving people in our world. The desire and potential for love is within us. Unfortunately, the overwhelming imperfections, evils, and problems within us and in the world surrounding us threaten to shatter our loving relationships at any given moment. Even though our hearts desire it, love often seems out of reach. However, because love is in our nature, we remain optimistic and continue to strive to learn and perfect it as much as possible. Still, is what humans can do enough to achieve a loving life and a loving world?

IF GOD IS THE SOURCE OF LOVE

The Bible tells us God is love (1 John 4:8). God's love is defined by who he is. One of the best definitions of God's love is seen in the person of Jesus, the Son of God. The Bible says Jesus is the exact representation of God (Hebrews 1:3), and Jesus said that to see him is to see God the Father (John 14:9). Therefore, when we understand from the Bible how Jesus and God the Father love each other and see how Jesus loves people, we are witnessing the definition of God's love. In Jesus' relationship with his Father, he knew that the Father loved him, and he loved others just as the Father loved him (John 15:9). Jesus was able to love because he had the love of the Father in himself. The Bible says that love comes from God (1 John 4:7). By doing the will of his Father (John 6:38), Jesus showed us and taught us what God's love is like. He did this by healing people, teaching God's truth to them (which many did not like), listening to them, encouraging them, accepting them, and forgiving them. God's presence and enabling power was with him. From Jesus we learn that acts of love require giving up something of one's own life to meet the needs of others. As Jesus said, "Greater love has no one than this, that one lay down his life for his friends" (John 15:13). When we see how Jesus loved, we are learning what God's kind of love is like; giving up one's own life for the good of another, even if one's life is threatened by such actions. Laying down one's life for another does not often mean physically dying for someone like Jesus did. It most often means dying to oneself by giving up one's comforts, interests, and selfish wants to give what another needs.

Although love involves voluntary actions, we know too that Jesus' works of love were not devoid of feelings. He was motivated often by his compassion for people (Mark 6:34; Luke 7:12-15). Jesus' love was at times recognized when people saw his tears (John 11:35-36; Luke 19:41-44). It is nice when feelings of love are present. Since people equate love with good feelings, we need to recognize not only that God has feelings but that there is a difference between God's feelings and ours. God loves with feelings such as compassion and even pain and sorrow as seen by his tears. However, his feelings, unlike ours, are not such that he is controlled by them, causing him to act rashly, inappropriately, and apart from right judgment and reasoning. When we read that God is angry, his anger is not to be equated with what we see in human anger. When God hates, his hate is not what we often think of in human terms. His anger and other feelings work to achieve what is right. We are often encouraged to put aside our anger because it is inappropriate and does not achieve the righteousness of God (James 1:19-20). Our feelings are often messed up and lead us in wrong directions. God's feelings are not messed up like ours, and they certainly do not take his acts of love in a wrong direction. Sometimes, because our feelings are not always appropriate or reliable, our love must act to do what's right, even if we don't feel like it. That is one reason God and Jesus command us to love, because love is an action that does what is right in the given situation, and as imperfect humans, the right feelings are not always there. To love God is to obey him and act in love as he would love (2 John 6).

STORIES OF GOD-LIKE LOVE

My wife and I spent a few days with a good friend whose wife had recently died. She had a debilitating disease and became unable to walk or feed herself, eventually losing her ability to communicate. In the last five years before she died, her husband, unable to leave her alone for long, was involved in caring for her needs. He shared with me a definition of love that he learned through his relationship with his wife. He said, "Love is when the other person's welfare and your welfare are very closely tied together." In other words, love is valuing people and caring about a person's welfare to the point of doing whatever it takes to meet the need. When the importance of people and their welfare is a part of who we are, the welfare of others is instinctively and voluntarily served. Furthermore, serving others improves our own well-being.

My friend likened love to the biblical story of the Good Samaritan told by Jesus in Luke 10:25-37. In that story a man wanted to know how to have the kind of life Jesus had and was told to love God with his whole being and to love his neighbor as himself. "Who is my neighbor?" the man asked. In other words, *Who should I love and not love?* Jesus told about an injured man lying alongside a road. Two men passed him by, perhaps because they had pressing things to do or had a prejudice against him. A third man stopped to help and took the man to a place where he could get the care he needed. Then Jesus asked a question: not, "Who is my neighbor?" but "Who was the neighbor to the injured man?" Rather than, *Who is my neighbor?*

the question is, *Who are you?* Are you the one who stops and shows mercy to one in need? Jesus said, "Go and do the same." In other words, love is not primarily based on human feelings that can so easily come and go or on one's tolerance or on a personal reason or condition that must be fulfilled. Rather, love is something you do because you are a loving person and there is a need. To love because that is who you are is God-like and easier said than done.

I heard of a test given to Christian students to see how they did with this definition of love. A poorly dressed man, obviously needing help, was sitting near a sidewalk where students attending a seminary were on their way to class. When they got to class, the professor asked them how many saw the man by the sidewalk. Hands were raised. "Who stopped to help?" he asked. They all passed by. A lesson was learned about the kind of love Jesus said to practice. It turns out that when any one of us has some place we are supposed to be, stopping to help someone is rare. My friend whose wife died defined love as being closely tied to another, with a heart that shares in that person's welfare. Love does something because there is a communal truth about love. Life involves interdependent relationships that connect and sustain us all. Interdependence means we need each other. A simple example is the grocer who provides food for your existence, and you buy it to aid his existence. Each of us in loving relationships must be willing to give to others and be open to receive from them what they have to give. Of course, there are times when stopping to help someone is not wise nor recommended. Being in touch with God helps us know when and how.

Another friend told me this story. He and his wife stopped at a fast food place while on a trip. There was a man outside, scantily dressed, not even properly covered. He followed them into the store and stayed with them as they approached the counter. They felt awkward and observed that no one in the restaurant seemed to notice the man, as if he was invisible to them. Later, as they resumed their travels, they talked and wondered if God had been there in the form of an angel, and they had ignored helping him. This experience so impacted them that they decided to get involved in one of their local organizations to help the poor.

JESUS TEACHES ABOUT LOVE

In addition to the story of the Good Samaritan, Jesus had more to teach about love. He told his followers to love their enemies and to pray for those who persecute them. God loves all people. Here is a paraphrase of something Jesus said: "Be perfect in love like your Father in heaven is perfect. If you love those who love you, what reward do you have? Do not even those you consider to be sinners do the same?" (Matthew 5:43-48, *paraphrase*). In both the Old and New Testaments of the Bible, God says to be kind to our enemies and help them (Proverbs 25:21-22; Romans 12:17-21). Jesus loved his enemies, even to the point of giving up his life for them so they could be forgiven and changed (Romans 5:6-11). God loves and cares for all people and wants all to be given the opportunity to discover his new and eternal life (Ezekiel 18:23, 32).

Forgiveness is another way Jesus says to love people and to be loved by people. We are to forgive others for their transgressions, even as God in Christ has forgiven us (Matthew 6:14-15; Ephesians 4:31-32; Colossians 3:12-14). In Matthew 18:21-35, Jesus told a story about forgiveness and its importance. In another story, Jesus shows how love and forgiveness are closely tied together. He said that those who are forgiven little, love little, and those who are forgiven much, love much (Luke 7:47). What we feel toward people who hurt us is usually not love but getting even. In a later chapter, we shall inquire into the many complicating aspects of love and forgiveness.

Loving as Jesus teaches can be extremely difficult, if not impossible, without divine input that changes our personhood. That is the point of divine love, for unlike human love, we love because God first loved us (1 John 4:19). Experiencing God's love transforms our lives and enables us to overcome many of the obstacles we as humans face in loving ourselves and others. The Apostle John tells us that love is from God, for God is love (1 John 4:7-8). Some would say, *I don't need God to be able to love others.* However, if it is true that God created us in his image, whether we believe in him or not, he is the one who instilled love in us and is therefore the true source of our ability to love. God sent Jesus to save the world, and he is humanity's best role model of love. For believers, being restored to his likeness is

24

our ultimate goal (Romans 8:29; 1 John 3:2-3; Philippians 3:20-21; 1 Timothy 1:5). We can't be Jesus, but with his Spirit living in us, which he provides (Luke 3:16; Acts 1:4-5), we can grow to be more like him.

A TEST OF YOUR LOVE

What does love involve? A lengthy definition of love in the Bible has sixteen character traits of God-likeness that we are to incorporate into our lives (1 Corinthians 13:1-8). On the left is the New American Standard Bible's wording (NASB); on the right are words from the New Living Translation Bible (NLT). Perhaps by using this definition of love, you can judge how you do at loving. Compare it to the love in each of your relationships. Obviously none of us will love perfectly, but it is good to have a target we can shoot for.

Love is patient.	Is patient
Love is kind.	Is kind
Love is not jealous.	Is not jealous
Love does not brag.	Is not boastful
Love is not arrogant.	Is not proud
Love does not act unbecomingly.	Is not rude
Love does not seek its own.	Does not demand its own way
Love is not provoked.	Is not irritable
Love does not take into account a wrong.	Keeps no record of being wronged
Love does not rejoice in unrighteousness.	Does not rejoice about injustice

25

Love rejoices with the truth.	Rejoices whenever the truth wins out
Love bears all things.	Never gives up
Love believes all things.	Never loses faith
Love hopes all things.	Is always hopeful
Love endures all things.	Endures through every circumstance
Love never fails. *(when other things do)*	Will last forever

God has given his people his Spirit of love (Romans 5:5) so that we can experience love and practice love as he wants. It may not be easy, but we can do better with God's help. By abiding in Christ (John 15:4-5) and walking in love as he loved us (Ephesians 5:1-2), we can keep growing in our love, becoming more and more like our Lord Jesus.

WHY WE DO NOT EXPERIENCE GOD'S LOVE

Already mentioned previously are the sinful acts of our human nature and the many human character defects that hinder love. Let me add to that list a few statements from the Bible of things that prevent us from experiencing God's love. First, we cannot serve two masters. We cannot worship God and something else. A heart divided cannot consistently experience and practice the love of God. If we love the world and the things in the world, then the love of God is not in us (Matthew 6:24; Mark 10:21-22; 2 Timothy 4:10; 1 John 2:15). Second, it is difficult to practice God's love when we love the approval of people more than the approval of God, and we follow what others want us to do (John 12:43; Acts 4:19-20). Third, Christians who claim belief in God can quench or grieve the Holy Spirit (Ephesian 4:25-32; 1 Thessalonians 5:19) and thus fail to love as God wants. Finally, we cannot experience God's love if we love the darkness rather than the light of truth (John 3:19-20). Jesus spoke of those who are unwilling to come to him and who are unwilling to hear his word and believe what he says (John 5:42-47).

Nevertheless, those who do not believe in God do experience aspects of his love, for God shows his kindness and sends his blessings on the evil and the good alike (Matthew 5:45; Luke 6:35; Acts 14:16-17). Humans who do not profess to know God are not only loved by God but are also able to practice his love. This is because they are created in God's image, and God has instilled within them his nature of love. However, humans will not know or admit that their love is from God because they do not acknowledge God (Romans 1:21), nor have they received within themselves the divine life of Jesus through his Spirit (John 1:11-13; 3:5-8). Although all humans have an inner sense that we ought to be loving people, we do not all have access to God's purity in our actions and motives, and that is why our human love, unaided by God's grace, in many ways falls short of what love is all about.

BECOMING A PERSON OF LOVE

I was with a few friends who were talking about the subject of food. One person made a remark that the additives that go into our food these days are not good for our health. Another agreed that these preservatives in our food are not good for us. One of the ladies in the group disagreed. "I'm getting older," she said, "and I need all the preservatives I can get." Laughter lightened the discussion, and in that moment, I thought to myself, *Actually, the greatest preservative for all of life is love; God's love.*

God's people are called to experience his love. To the churches in Rome, God said, "We overwhelmingly conquer through Christ who loved us because nothing can separate us from his love" (Romans 8:37-39). To the churches in Corinth, God says concerning faith, hope, and love, that "the greatest of these is love" (1 Corinthians 13:13). He also said it is the love of Christ that controls us so that we who live might no longer live for ourselves but for him who died and rose again on our behalf (2 Corinthians 5:14-15). To the church in Galatia, God says, "Through love serve one another" (Galatians 5:13-14). To the church at Ephesus, God says, "Walk in love, just as Christ also loved you" (Ephesians 5:2). To the church at Philippi, God says he wants their "love to abound still more and more in real knowledge and all discernment" (Philippians 1:9). To the church at Colossae, God says, "Beyond all these things, put on love, which is the perfect bond of unity" (Colossians 3:14). To the Thessalonian church, a prayer is, "May the Lord cause you to increase and abound in love for one another, and for all people, just as we also do for you" (1 Thessalonians 3:12). To Timothy, a leader in the church, God says, "The goal of our instruction is love from a pure heart" (1 Timothy 1:5). To the Hebrew Christians, God says, "Let love of the brethren continue," and "Let us consider how to stimulate one another to love and good deeds" (Hebrews 13:1; 10:24).

Peter, an apostle of the Lord, says to the churches, "Above all, keep fervent in your love for one another, because love covers a multitude of sins" (1 Peter 4:8). John, another apostle of Jesus, says, "If God so loved us, we ought to love one another" (1 John 4:11). Jude says, "Beloved, building yourselves up on your most holy faith, praying in the Holy Spirit, keep yourselves in the love of God" (Jude 1:20-21). In the Old Testament, God lets everyone know that he is a God of lovingkindness and that his people are to love God and to love their neighbor as themselves (Exodus 34:6:7; Psalm 89:14; Deuteronomy 6:5; Leviticus 19:18). Jesus said, "This is my commandment, that you love one another, just as I have loved you" (John 15:12). He also said that people would know we are his disciples by how we love one another (John 13:35). Love is doing good by meeting human needs with a godly motive. This doing of good is how evil in the world is overcome (Romans 12:21).

In the beginning, God breathed into man the breath of life, and he became a living soul. Breathing is a natural function in our daily lives. We inhale to breathe in and exhale to breathe out. The love between the Father and Jesus was like that. Jesus continuously spent time with God, inhaling the Father's love and then exhaling that love out to others. We do the same. Each day, as we fellowship with Jesus (1 John 1:3), as we take in and hear his words, God breathes his love into us. Then we do as Jesus did and breathe it out to others.

CONCLUDING, BUT NOT EXHAUSTIVE, DEFINITION OF LOVE

Most of the statements about love in this chapter define some dimension of what love is or does. Love is the place where we are not alone, where we are the safest, where we are most valued, and on and on. The source of love is the key to how deeply we can experience love and how successfully we can give it. Experiencing God's love purifies our lives so that the loving actions we do, when done in the power of his Holy Spirit, are without the taint of sinful or selfish motives but are sacrificially given for imparting the goodness of God to others. Love is like an energy that flows into us and through us to others. Scientists tell us that objects in our world need a source of energy to maintain them. In fact, everything needs to be connected to an energy source. For example, our computers and phones, if left to themselves, lose energy and die out. We must plug them in to an energy source that keeps them going. Our physical lives require the same. Food is an energy source, and we must eat to keep living. There must be data in for there to be data out—input for there to be output. The same is true with love. As we remain connected to God as our energy source for love, we can continue operating and giving love out. Some think humans, left to their own resources, can adequately love without God. Look around at our world and at your own life. How are we doing? Love works best in an imperfect world like ours when we are connected to a perfect, never dying, love source. Therefore, I define what love is as follows.

> *Love is a person. That person is the God who is Father, Son, and Holy Spirit.*
>
> *Love is what that person says it is. Love is what that person says to do.*
>
> *Love is infinite; there is no end to that person's love, and its depths for us are worth finding out.*
>
> *Love is admitting God into one's life and experiencing being loved by God.*

Love is giving to all others, including oneself, the love we have received from God.

Paul prayed, "May the Lord direct your hearts into the love of God" (2 Thessalonians 3:5). What would happen if you and I continuously prayed, and prayed at moments of need, "Lord, direct my heart into your love"? What might God do in and through us?

CHAPTER 2

LOVE'S ROLL IN OVERCOMING LIFE'S PROBLEMS

I came home one day and said to my wife, "Everybody on this planet is in some kind of battle with some kind of a problem, or multiple problems, and they are fighting for survival." I made this statement because I had just come home from listening to another person's problems that were so heartbreaking, I felt at a loss to know how to help. I made this statement having recently received news of an acquaintance diagnosed with a dreaded disease that involves a fight for one's life. I made this statement having learned about a little girl continually being sexually abused by her father. This little girl faces horrific trauma and potential feelings of guilt, worthlessness, abandonment, mistrust of people, and anger over injustice.

Suffering surrounds us. I know how burdensome, fearful, and life-threatening my own problems can feel. With certain problems, we can't help but experience disturbing emotions, restlessness, and sleepless nights. Hopelessness, fears, and sorrows lead to anxiety, despair, and a deep inner sickening sense that our life is falling apart. Many feel like they can't endure their situation, and they want to run away—some do, even to the point of suicide. These feelings are real and are indicators that something is terribly wrong and needs to be righted. If not resolved, our problems destroy us.

When Jesus said, "Every day will have enough trouble of its own" (Matthew 6:34) and proclaimed, "In the world you have tribulation" (John 16:33), he was telling us that we will all face difficult times. Jesus himself experienced seemingly insurmountable afflictions and sufferings (Isaiah 53:3; 2 Corinthians 1:5). At various times, everyone—rich, poor, or in between—battles some kind of a problem that to some degree threatens their well-being. The problem might be how to raise kids to survive in a dangerous and unpredictable world, paying bills, overcoming bad habits and addictions, trying to make a relationship work, getting an education to better one's life, trying to find a job, seeking ways to escape poor conditions, or wishing someone would love them. People desperately need hope, healing, comfort, and peace.

Whoever came up with the phrase *survival of the fittest,* whether Charles Darwin, Herbert Spencer, or someone else, they were right in recognizing this undeniable condition of the world we live in. Every lifeform, from plants to animals to humans, is presented with troublesome situations that necessitate the need for survival, and it is the fittest that are able to overcome the problems and survive. When it comes to humans, an important question to ask is this, *What enables us to be fit enough to overcome our world of troubles?*

TWO PATHS FOR OVERCOMING PROBLEMS

"The Road Not Taken" was written by American poet Robert Frost. In his poem, he came to a place where the road on which he was traveling split into two, and he had to decide which road to take. In the end, after lengthy thought, he said that he "took the one less traveled by, and that has made all the difference." Frost is saying that we come to times in our lives when we must choose between two paths. It can be a tough choice, but the path we choose determines in large measure the outcome of our life. The battles you and I face bring us to a place of having to decide what path will make us fit enough to overcome our troubles.

Biblical writers also recognized two paths. A psalm writer considered two paths long ago when he said, "Do not trust in princes, in mortal man, in whom there is no salvation . . . how blessed is he whose help is the God of Jacob, whose hope is in the Lord his God" (Psalm 146:3-5). The prophet Jeremiah said the same: "Cursed is the man who trusts in mankind and makes flesh his strength, and whose heart turns away from the Lord. Blessed is the man who trusts in the Lord and whose trust is the Lord" (Jeremiah 17:5, 7). Jesus spoke of two paths when he said that one leads to destruction and the other to life (Matthew 7:13-14). Jesus said few find the one that leads to life. One path is a choice to go a human way, and the other path is a choice to go a superhuman way. Although humans can and do help one another with various degrees of success, for me, I choose to travel the supernatural path, the way of Christ Jesus. His way also includes the help of others, for God works through people. I am aware of reasons some people feel God is non-existent or unreliable as a source of help, and I respect their choice. No matter which path we choose, it's important to consider the extent and depth of the problems we face and the kind of help we need. I am betting that for most, Christ's way is the road less traveled. Before choosing your path, it is worth taking a long look at each one: the human path and God's path.

THE HUMAN PATH

There is no doubt that we humans possess skills and abilities to accomplish great and magnificent things in all areas of life, including the use of imagination and reason in solving difficult problems. Scientific discoveries in all fields of knowledge are adding to our ability to provide help for individuals and our world. Although the problems people experience are many and varied, an increasing number of people admit their need for help and are willing to get it. Seeking mental health counselors, buying self-help books, using medications, and being interested in spirituality or religions of all kinds, shows that individuals want to overcome their problems and have a better life. People try anything and everything that promises to help them, and they keep trying things until they find something that works. No doubt people do find help and relief in many of the things they try. Certainly, my goal is not to put down any well-intentioned source of help that comes from people who genuinely want to help others. Truths that work may be found in any source of help, and application of those truths to our hurting lives can effectively contribute to our wholeness. I come back, however, to the question, *Which path will make us fit enough to overcome life's troubling issues?* All the human efforts I have just mentioned are helpful, but are they enough?

Regarding the human path, there is a problem with the belief that humans can fix the world. We fail to see and acknowledge the depth of the many kinds of evil in this world and how insurmountable the problems are. For example, human imperfections contribute greatly to our inability to defeat the problems that plague us. We fail to take into account the extent of negative thoughts and attitudes, life-destroying habits and addictions, uncontrolled anger, greed, and many other immoral behaviors, all of which prevent us from attaining a problem-free life and world. Because we fail to see the extent and depth of evil in and around us, we are deceived into thinking that we as humans are strong enough to fight and overcome this world's problems. We do find a way to win a battle or two, and things seem to go along smoothly for a while, so it appears that we are capable of winning all the time. But do humans have the ability to overcome the overwhelming amount of adversity in this world? If we humans are so good at fixing our problems, why is police protection needed all over the world? If we are so good at fixing our problems, why do so many of our tried solutions fail to work as we had hoped? Does the condition of this world look like we are able to fix our problems?

How *are* we humans doing in defeating our problems? Life is often so disheartening that many become stressed and depressed. Many fall into debilitating pits such as guilt and shame, self-pity, anger, fear, anxiety, mental craziness, or hopelessness, and they despair when they see no way out. It seems that divisions among people—whether in our homes, our nation, or the world—frequently escalate to the point that it takes the control of government, a war, or separation from each other to bring order and peace. These are obvious signs that our problems are defeating us. Unfortunately, humans become convinced that we can win any battle. Unwilling to admit pride, even in a losing battle, the human way is to keep fighting, thinking we can and will win. Even if we fail, our pride can make us unwilling to admit our faults, and we tend to blame someone or something else for what is happening or has happened.

As we travel on the human path, there is no doubt we humans have a strong will and desire to want to overcome our problems and survive all obstacles. That is why humans do everything they can to protect themselves from threats to their well-being. Unfortunately, if we can't overcome our problems by being good and doing what's right, we may be tempted to give in to wrong ways to win. We may stoop to lying, cheating, stealing, and even destroying the lives of others to save ourselves and survive. Certainly, we underestimate the extent of evils in the world, and our many self-centered ways help create our problems. I am not saying there is no good in us and in the world, only that it is too limited to be able to create a pain-free and peaceful world. Underestimation of the evils we face causes us to overestimate our ability to save ourselves. In the next few paragraphs, we examine three primary reasons why people reject God's path.

How Humans View the Super-Human Path

One reason for rejecting God's path is the belief of some that we humans are capable of overcoming our problems and can make the world into a better place without God. I think we humans are amazing in the good things we can achieve. However, why is that? It occurs to me that if there is a supreme God who is good, who is devoid of evil, and who made humans in his image, and I believe there is, then humans are capable of doing the things they do because they were created and endowed with the reasoning, creativity, and morality of their Creator. That being the case, they are simply doing, at least in part, what a good God created them to be and do. To say they don't need God to make the world a better place fails to realize that in fact they are using the powers and skills given them by God to try to make it happen. Are we not deceived and arrogant to think that, apart from God, we are accomplishing all the great

35

things we do? The Apostle Paul, talking to philosophical thinkers of Athens, Greece, said that they were ignorant of the fact that we all are children of God by creation, and that "in him we live, move, and exist" (Acts 17:26-30). Prophets of old proclaimed that arrogance has deceived us into thinking we humans can be our own god (Obadiah 1:3; Jeremiah 49:16).

Second, people reject God's path because it is not popular, nor proper, in our pluralistic world to say that Jesus is the only answer to our problems. Pluralistic thinkers say that Christianity is just one of many valid religions and should not be elevated above others. Christians believe that Jesus is the only way. Those outside the faith say it is rude and arrogant for Christians to imply that other beliefs are wrong and the Christian way is right. I am not denying that helpful truths can be learned from other religions and philosophies, but is it not true that a comparative study of religions reveals that Jesus is certainly unique, in that he has said and done things that no one else has ever said or done? What is wrong, then, with saying that his claims and powers clearly stand out above others (John 2:18-22)? If his teachings and powers, like raising dead people to life, are unique, why not listen to him and consider anything he has to offer that might be above-and-beyond the offerings of other religions? If Superman were a real person in our world instead of a fictional character, would we not rely on him for help over others who claimed to be super but who could not demonstrate it by their powers and deeds? The truth is that people hate being told what is or is not appropriate for them, or that they are sinful; so when Jesus tells people those things, they reject or kill him (Mark 11:15-18; John 3:19-20; 8:37-47).

A third reason people reject the God path is that they try it, and it fails them. Those on the human path, when they finally meet a problem they can't overcome by their own efforts, do often choose religion or a god to rely on as a source of power. But is their religion and their god real and able to save them? I've met people who told me they tried Jesus and it did not work, so naturally, they dismiss him as an option for their survival. Is that because Jesus was only a religion they were trying? The truth is that many people who turn to God or religion to save them are actually depending on themselves.

If they obey the rules of the religion or god of their choice, they believe they will be rewarded. They are still trying to be in control of their own destinies, using God and religion as a way to get what they want. Naturally, if religion, including Jesus, doesn't give them what they want, they will look for other ways to defeat the problems that are destroying their world of peace and security. Actually, there is no reason to stick with Jesus if we fail to grasp who he is and how the salvation he offers works. If religion is not working, and bad things are happening to us, it is easy to criticize God for being mean and punishing, or for leaving us to suffer and not helping us. I agree with this statement made by psychotherapist Larry Crabb: "We don't worship God; we try to use Him, and then angrily dismiss Him when He proves unhelpful."[4]

Is there anyone, other than ourselves or other humans, who can save us from the destructive words, behaviors, and problems of this world? A corrupted human race cannot stop from doing wrong and hurtful things to ourselves and to others (Romans 7:18-19, 24). Because of those wrong and hurtful things, we need freedom from guilt as well as from feelings of shame, loneliness, and self-condemnation. We need help to overcome the worries and fears and paranoid thoughts that oppress and depress us. Ultimately, we need to know and feel that we are loved, protected, and safe from the many evils that threaten to ruin our lives, destroy our peace, and take away hope in a good future. As humans, we need to know that we belong to someone who cares about us no matter what we have ever said or done and that we are loved and accepted without fear of love going away. What can a loving God do for us that humans or religion cannot do?

GOD'S PATH

Christianity, as is true with other religious or spiritual movements, claims to have the answer for our human predicaments (Romans 8:38-39). Actually, Christians claim Jesus is the answer not because they are trying to be controlling or arrogant but because Jesus is the one who claims it (John 10:10). We humans know something

---

4. Larry Crabb, *The Safest Place on Earth* (Nashville, TN: W Publishing Group, a division of Thomas Nelson Inc, 1999), 136.

is wrong, and we know how we wish things to be, but that does not mean we see our problems correctly or know what to do about them. Christians too, like non-Christians, are easily blinded to their real problems and needs (2 Peter 1:9; 1 John 2:11; Revelation 3:17); or we ignore them, not wanting to face them (John 3:19-21). We focus, instead, on surface wants and wishes.

Jesus came to help us see what is really going on in the world and in us (John 9:39-41). God knows what we really need, and he offers insight through his Word, the Bible. If we were willing to understand and accept what God says about us, we would find out that our primary underlying problem is that we are self-centered beings who most often put our own interests above God's or others' (Mark 8:33; Philippians 2:4, 21). For our own comfort and good, we try to make things happen the way we want them to be rather than the way God wants them to be.

I have a friend who believes in God and Jesus, but his belief was not helping him overcome his problems. Here is how he described his life to me:

> Though I believed in God and Jesus, I was living with addictions. Mine was alcohol, but there are many others we addictive people can be trapped in—it could be greed, gambling, drugs, pornography, anything. Our addictions take us away from the Lord. Our family suffers, our friendships suffer, and our livelihood suffers. Our ability to love and care as Jesus wants is non-existent. Our human relationships end with some sort of pain, maybe poor health, no security, lack of self-worth, even mental illness. Why? Because we stop caring for others to live for that which is evil, believing it makes us feel good. Ultimately, we hate what we've become. This causes those who love us great pain and suffering.

My friend is very grateful that, through the prolonged help of fellow believers and God, he came to understand and unravel the problems that plagued his life. He discovered love's role in overcoming life's problems.

The truth is that Jesus came to destroy evil and is the only one who can truly heal us and guarantee a peaceful future (1 John 3:8;

Isaiah 53:5; Acts 4:12). Humans need a strong inner or central core within their being, something that will hold their lives together and keep them from falling apart under the stress of their problems. The deeper we experience and trust the love of Jesus, the more at peace we are in the midst of our problems, and the more certain we are that everything will be all right. I am learning that being loved by the world's greatest power for good is what enables me not to feel alone and that being loved provides the safest place to be in the midst of a life-threatening world. Following are seven ways Jesus loves us, thus becoming for us the one who provides "love's role in overcoming life's problems":

SEVEN WAYS WE EXPERIENCE THE LOVE OF JESUS

(1) HIS SACRIFICE

How does Jesus love us? *He sacrifices his own comforts to meet our needs.* Motivated by his Father's love for the world, and out of concern for our well-being, Jesus laid aside his position and privileges as God and left the safety of his heavenly realm. He became human like us and did his Father's will, even to the point of suffering death to rescue us from our corrupted lives and world (Philippians 2:6-9; 2 Peter 1:4). The Apostle John said, "We know love by this, that he laid down his life for us" (1 John 3:16). Jesus himself said, "Greater love has no one than this, that one lay down his life for his friends" (John 15:13). "I am the good shepherd," he said, and "I lay down my life for the sheep" (John 10:11, 15). Those who saw and lived with Jesus testify that "God has sent his only begotten son into the world so that we might live through him. In this is love, not that we loved God, but that he loved us and sent his Son to be the propitiation for our sins" (1 John 4:9-10). The Apostle Paul said, "God demonstrates his own love toward us, in that while we were yet sinners, Christ died for us" (Romans 5:8). The prophet Isaiah spoke of Jesus when he said, "He was pierced through for our transgressions," and "Each of us has turned to his own way; but the Lord has caused the iniquity of us all to fall on him" (Isaiah 53:5-6). And the Apostle Peter said, "He himself bore our sins in his body on the cross . . . for by his wounds, you were healed" (1 Peter 2:24). The voluntary willingness to give up his life to save ours is how Jesus loved us.

Here is how I came to know and believe his love for me and how it met vital needs in my life. I needed to be saved from the awful, panic-stricken fear of death I was under. I invited him into my life because he said he is the resurrection and the life, and all who believe in him will never die. He came into me, and by experiencing the assurance of eternal life, I have experienced his love firsthand. And furthermore, over time, he has been changing me into a new person. One day, I realized my sinfulness is the reason he suffered on the cross. I visualized his suffering and pain, and I felt that I had put him there; it brought me to tears. Because of what he did, I know he forgives all my wrongs, and I am free from all guilt. With much gratitude, I owe him my life. I am one of his new creations (2 Corinthians 5:17). I am a child of God and supremely loved by him (1 John 3:1-2). Knowing we are loved and accepted is perhaps the deepest need in the heart of humankind.

(2) HIS TEACHING

How does Jesus love us? *He teaches us.* While on earth, he taught like no one else; he taught with authority (Matthew 7:28-29). He doesn't quote well-known and respected persons who agree with him as a way to back up his teachings. He wasn't like the prophets before him who credited the Lord God as the source of their messages. The authority of what Jesus teaches resides in himself. He refers to himself as one with God. He backed up the authority of what he said by miraculous works (Mark 2:1-13). This infuriated the religious teachers of his day because, being a man, he was making himself out to be God (John 5:18; 10:22-39; 19:4-12). When Jesus taught about God's Law in the Old Testament, he said things like, "You may have heard it said, but I say unto you . . ." (Matthew 5:21-30). Jesus claims to be the ultimate authority on what he teaches. He not only teaches the truth (John 8:51), but he claims, "I am the truth" (John 14:6). People flocked to hear his teachings, whether at the seashore (Mark 2:13), on a mountain (Matthew 5-7), or in the temple (John 7:28-31; 8:2). Disciples who personally heard his teachings recorded them, and they are forever preserved for all generations in what we now call the Bible (1 John 1:1-5).

When I read the Bible and hear his teachings, I realize his teaching is an act of his guiding love. He wants me to know things I can learn from no other source. He teaches me how to have life eternal and how to have a life that leads to happiness and peace (Matthew 5:1-12). His words sustain and protect me from being led in a wrong and destructive direction; they help me avoid the errant and dangerous ways of this world. I can recognize the truth of other people's teachings by comparing them to Jesus' teachings. If they are in opposition, I can be saved from teachings that may sound good but will eventually lead me astray (Proverbs 14:12; 16:25; Colossians 2:8; 2 Corinthians 10:5). When I feel confused and at a loss to know what to think or do, I know that his words will give me direction that I can absolutely trust. They bring me out of darkness and into the light of truth (John 8:12; 8:31-32, 45-47). I derive my worldview from the Word of God.

(3) HOPE

How does Jesus love us? *He loves us by giving us hope.* The hope he gives helps us overcome fear in the face of the troubling problems of our world. Jesus lets us know what we can expect in the future, assures us that he has overcome all problems of this world, and guarantees our participation in his victory in the end (John 16:33; 14:27; Romans 8:31-39; 1 Corinthians 6:14; Revelation 5:9-10; 21:1-5). God is a God of hope (Romans 15:13). Believing the certainty of his hope enables us to have joy, comfort, and peace in the midst of personal problems and fearful world conditions. Hope involves everything future, all his promises, and his prophecies yet to be fulfilled. The Lord's promises and prophecies are what we hang on to until his help arrives to heal and complete us, whether now in this life or when he comes again.

One of the books I wrote in this three-book series is about hope. I use the example of a sports fan watching a game and wanting his team to win. Not knowing if they will, he experiences all kinds of emotions during the game. He may feel joyful, disappointed, angry, upset, worried, hopeful, fearful, dejected, and so forth. Sometimes I watch a game that has already happened, has been recorded, and I know how it ends. When I watch it, I do not go through all those up and down emotions because I know how the game ends. In the same way, when I have upset emotions due to life's uncertain circumstances, I can work through them and come to peace when I know what God promises and how life ends. His presence and promises give us hope.

(4) BEARING OUR BURDENS

How does Jesus love us? *He helps bear our burdens and lightens the weight of them so that we can get through them* (Matthew 11:28-30). Here are three examples of how he helps bear our burdens. First, we can call on him to come into any situation and have him impact how it goes. I was sitting with a group of people, feeling irritated by their obscene talk. I felt out of place in this situation and under a weight of growing anger. I remember sitting there and pleading for God to give me a heart of love so that I could enter into the conversation with a good spirit. My feelings changed, and I no longer felt irritated and angry. I actually was relaxed and had a meaningful relational time with the group. The second example involves those times I am facing difficult situations and my heart is deeply troubled. I go to the Bible, and his Word gives me wisdom to deal with the situation and a peace that calms my spirit. Many are comforted with verses like Isaiah 41:10 which says, "Do not fear, for I am with you; Do not anxiously look about you, for I am your God. I will strengthen you, surely I will help you." A third way he helps lighten our burdens is through other people. The Law of Christ is love, and when we see or hear of someone in need, he teaches us to fulfill his love by bearing one another's burdens (Galatians 6:2). We are encouraged to act and become the love of Jesus to others, and they become the love of Jesus to us.

(5) ADMONITION

How does Jesus love us? *He loves us by admonishing us when we get off the path.* He corrects our thinking and behaviors as needed. We see it in the ways he corrects his disciples. Sometimes, when his disciples are afraid in a situation, he will ask them, "Where is your faith?" (Luke 8:25), or "You of little faith, why did you doubt?" (Matthew 14:31). One time his disciples wanted to get revenge and kill others, but Jesus rebuked them and said, "You do not know what kind of spirit you are of; for the son of man did not come to destroy men's lives, but to save them" (Luke 9:55-56). One time, when asked by Jesus to pray about a situation, his disciples did not pray, and he said, "Could you not have watched with me for one hour? Keep watching and praying that you may not enter into temptation; for the spirit is willing, but the flesh is weak" (Matthew 26:40-41). When Peter argued against something Jesus said, Jesus responded, "Get behind me, Satan; for you are not setting your mind on God's interests, but man's" (Mark 8:31-33). Jesus, by his Spirit who lives within us, or through reading his Word, often corrects our thinking or behaviors. I remember when I would not forgive someone, and his voice within me said, *I thought you were a Christian, how can you hate that person?* There have been many times when an inner voice reminded me that I was not on love's path. He may also use other people to admonish us (Romans 15:14).

(6) HIS KINDNESS

How does Jesus love us? *He is kind and good to us by meeting our needs, at times surprising us by unexpected happenings that show he cares for us.* I have many stories of things God has done for me, sometimes in answer to prayer and sometimes without expecting it. I remember as a child folding a paper airplane, and it would not fly. I prayed for God to help it fly, and the next time I threw it, it floated beautifully across the room. I was amazed, and it helped me believe in God. Another way God showed his kindness and goodness was by the circumstances that clearly led my wife and I to live out our life's vocational calling in Montana. I suppose God knew my love for nature and my wife's need for good health; but mostly, he knew where we would fit well with the people he wanted us to be in ministry with. We were very grateful he led us there. All through my life, there have been incidents that most people would call coincidence, chance, good luck, or destiny. There is, however, no doubt in my heart and mind that these happenings are providential signs of the love, care, kindness, and goodness that God shows to all people. An example of this occurs in the story of the Ethiopian riding in a chariot, heading home. Reading the scroll of Isaiah, he could not understand its meaning until God surprised him be sending Phillip, who helped him understand what he was reading (Acts 8:26-40). Christians and non-Christians alike experience God's kind acts in meeting their needs (Matthew 5:45; Romans 2:4). Much more will be said about this in chapter eight on God's providential love.

(7) HIS EXAMPLE

How does Jesus love us? *He loves us by being an example of how to live.* He is a good example of a humble servant, not proud and self-promoting, but a person who gives himself to meet needs. In humbling himself to wash his disciples' feet, he showed that he was not here to boss people around against their wills, but to serve others (John 13:1-17; Luke 22:24-27). Jesus even washed the feet of Judas, his betrayer and enemy. Jesus' humility was also demonstrated by his example of suffering for the sake of others, even to the point of death (1 Peter 2:19-25; Philippians 2:4-8). He did not exist to please himself only but to please others and do good for them (Romans 15:1-3; Acts 10:38). There is no better role model for us.

In summary, the Lord loves you and me exactly as we need to be loved. He loves me by sacrificing his life for me so I can have life and have it abundantly (John 10:10). He loves me by teaching me what life is all about—things I need to learn to keep me well-grounded on the path to a good and blessed life (Matthew 5:1-10; 7:24-25). He loves me by giving me the hope that he is with me daily and guarantees me an eternal future with him and my fellow believers in a perfect new world (John 14:1-3). He loves me by always being with me to help bear my burdens and get me through tough times (Matthew 11:28-30). He gives encouragement to help me persevere and sends people to help me. He loves me by correcting my thoughts and behaviors so I can become a better person and share in his holiness (Hebrews 12:5-11). He loves me by things he does in the circumstances of daily life to help me and to prove that he cares about me (Romans 8:28-29). He loves me by being a good example and model for me to follow so I can become wise, loving, and good like him (Luke 6:40). When we experience the ways Jesus loves us, his love for us sinks deeper into our soul. Such love draws us close to him, and because we know he cares for us, we cast all our anxieties on him (1 Peter 5:7).

CONCLUDING THOUGHTS

Experiencing God's love is the starting point in overcoming our problems. Believers are to follow the admonition of Jude to "keep yourself in the love of God" (Jude 1:21). We keep ourselves in his love by reading and practicing his Word daily and by being reminded of how valuable we are to him as a person he created and is saving. We can know deep down in our soul that he loves us. Experiencing his love calms our fears and strengthens us in the midst of difficulties. The biblical book of Romans says that when we are loved by God, nothing, not even death, can destroy us or separate us from him and the life he promises. Romans 8:31-39 mentions many problems humans face, encouraging us with these words: "But in all these things we overwhelmingly conquer through him who loved us."

The Bible says, "The name of the Lord is a strong tower; the righteous runs into it and is safe" (Proverbs 18:10). We experience this on a human level. For example, my wife and I were at our grandson's high school graduation party when a visiting neighbor with a large hyperactive dog came up on the back deck of the house where we had gathered. Our five-year-old-grandson, afraid of the dog, ran screaming in terror to his dad. What do you think happened to him when he got to his dad? He became calm, and his fear was gone. He felt safe and received comforting assurance that everything would be all right. He ran into the loving arms of his dad because he knew his dad had the power to protect him and keep him safe. Those who believe in the love of Jesus are invited to do the same thing with him and experience the same results. When we encounter problems, running to him, experiencing his love and being strengthened to re-enter life's ventures, needs to become our default position.

I know what many may be thinking. *Jesus does not always protect people who run to him, for they may die.* That is true. Again, we look to the example of Jesus. Even though his Father loved him, and Jesus loved his Father, yet Jesus was killed by those who were against him. How did his Father's love help him? Jesus knew many things about the love of God that comforted and strengthened him, even in his death. He knew that others could kill his body but not his soul and that God valued him and would take care of him, so he was not afraid (Matthew 10:28-31). He knew that God would judge those who wronged him. Justice would be done, and so he did not have to hate others and feel vengeful (1 Peter 2:23). He knew God had a good reason for the bad things that were happening to him (Isaiah 53:5-6, 10-11; Hebrews 2:10, 14-15). He knew that God would take care of those loved ones he left behind (John 14:16-18; 19:26-27). Although he may have felt that God abandoned him, he never lost faith and hope in God's promises (Psalm 22:1-5, 19-20; Luke 23:46). He knew God would resurrect his body (Psalm 16:9-10; Mark 8:31). He knew his loving Father was present with him and so was not shaken by his afflictions (Psalm 16:8; Acts 2:25-28). He knew that an evil-free world awaited him and that many fellow humans would share it with him. This gave him joy and helped him endure his sufferings (Hebrews 12:2).

Followers of Jesus must grow in experiencing the truth that says, "We have come to know and have believed the love which God has for us" (1 John 4:16). To know and believe God's love provides for us a strong inner core and is where the ability to overcome our problems begins.

CHAPTER 3

UNDERSTANDING THE GOD OF LOVE

Jesus said that God is a Spirit, and he wants us to relate to him in spirit and in truth (John 4:24). We might put it this way: he wants us to relate to him with our heart and mind, for Jesus also said that God is a loving God who wants us to love him with our whole being, heart, soul, and mind (Matthew 22:37). God is a personal God who wants a personal relationship with us. God not only tells us who he is, he also tells us who we are. Why would we want, or need, to understand the God of love? The answer is that misunderstandings and faulty ideas about God and ourselves can prevent us from knowing God and truly experiencing God's love. How could we possibly have a good, honest, truthful, right, and loving relationship with God without understanding one another?

What keeps us from knowing and understanding God? Maybe we reject God because of bad experiences. For example, a loved one may have died, and God did not answer our prayers as we wanted, or, we may know followers of God who are hypocritical, and this turns us off to wanting to know their God. Those who have access to a Bible may get wrong views of God due to superficial readings, misinterpretations, or unanswered questions. Consider also that the world is full of peoples' gods, all of these gods differing from each other as well as from the biblical God of love. Worshipping those gods is likely to lead away from the God of love. Misunderstandings of God are often due to unawareness, human philosophies, lack of interest, the culture we are brought up in, family traditions, personal prejudices, or things we read or hear from a variety of sources, or we are set in our ways and have closed minds. If we are to understand the God of love, we need to know how he communicates who he is to us. And even if we do not want to know him, it is good to know who he is so we are not rejecting him out of ignorance or wrong reasons. That would be unfair to him and us.

THE GOD OF LOVE MAKES HIMSELF KNOWN

Are humans the deciders of who God is? Or, has the God of love spoken and explained himself to us? If so, are we letting him explain himself? If we want others to know who we are, we must be able to communicate things about ourselves to them, and they need to hear and understand us. If the God of love has revealed things about himself, we can come to know God and what God is like. The question is, am I willing to open myself up to the ways God speaks? If so, we will discover that he has spoken in a variety of ways, all of which help us grow in our understanding of what kind of God he is. Following are five ways the God of love makes himself known.

First, he is known through Jesus, who was with God, who was God, and who became a man (John 1:1-2, 14; Philippians 2:5-8). One day Jesus said to a group of people, "You are from below; I am from above. You are of this world; I am not of this world" (John 8:23). Jesus was sent by God to accomplish God's purposes and to explain who God is (John 1:18; Hebrews 1:1-3). Jesus said that if you have seen him, you have seen the Father (John 14:9-10). Jesus is revealed throughout a historically trustworthy Bible in which he shows and tells us what God is like.

Second, God has spoken to us through the very scriptures Jesus believed in and lived by. Jesus said that we should not live on bread alone but on every word that proceeds out of the mouth of God (Matthew 4:4). The scriptures contain God's messages that were God-breathed by his Spirit into his Old Testament prophets and into his New Testament apostles (Hebrews 1:1; 2 Timothy 3:15-17; John 14:25-26; 2 Peter 1:16-21; 1 John 1:1-5). Through these messages, God tells us who he is and what he is doing to restore his world.

Third, God has revealed himself through historical events caused by him and witnessed by people on earth. God's acts in history include providential circumstances he works out to achieve his purposes (Joseph's life, Genesis 50:15-21; the book of Esther), miraculous events such as parting the Red Sea (Joshua 2:10-11), and prophesied events that came true—for example, the resurrection of Jesus from the dead (Psalm 16:10; Mark 8:31). Many of these acts of God, recorded throughout the Bible, are supported by a verification of the facts from archaeological discoveries.[5] Furthermore, there are people today who testify to acts of God which they have witnessed.

Fourth, "His invisible attributes, his eternal power and divine nature, have been clearly seen, being understood through what has been made" (Romans 1:20). If any of us were to make something, the things we make would tell others something about ourselves, even though they had never seen us. God tells us things about himself through the natural world he created. For example, discovery that the earth has many finely tuned factors necessary to sustain life demonstrates something the Bible says—that the earth was made to be inhabited. The implication is clear that the Maker is intelligent, is powerful, and cares about living things, especially humans.

Fifth, God is known through the witness of people he helps and indwells by his Holy Spirit (Matthew 5:14-16; Titus 2:11-14; 1 Peter 2:9). I see and learn to know God through my personal relationship with him, by hearing persons talk about their experiences with God, and by seeing how he changes people from who they had been into persons with undying faith, hope, and love. People can be turned off by Christians who are not good witnesses. That is understandable,

---

5. On the internet, type in "Patterns of Evidence Series," an interesting series by filmmaker Timothy Mahoney. See *Patterns of Evidence: The Exodus* and *Patterns of Evidence: The Red Sea Miracle* (Parts 1 & 2), as well as other information.

but not all believers can be put in the same category. Many are genuine; they live in line with God's character and teachings, and their life is attractive to us (1 Thessalonians 1:2-10; Ephesians 2:1-10). No one is perfect, and even unbelievers are often hypocritical. Christians make no claim for perfection but only a claim for a God who is perfect, who loves and forgives them.

When we want to know more of who God is or find answers to questions about him, these are five sources we can consult. The most complete information about the God of love is found in the scriptures; however, putting together all of the ways he makes himself known provides a more complete picture of him. Furthermore, if God expects us to believe in him, all the ways he uses to reveal himself must be truthful and coherent—that is, they will be in agreement so as not to leave us conflicted due to contradictions. For example, what science observes about nature will not contradict the Bible, and vice versa, because God is the Author of both, and if both are interpreted correctly, they will agree. It is true, there are things about God that seem contradictory, but to him they are not. For example, how can Jesus be both God and man, or how can there be free will when God determines things, or how can his love be both conditional and unconditional? Obviously we will never be able to know or understand God completely, for he is infinite, and we are not (Deuteronomy 29:29; Isaiah 55:8-9). However, from the various sources God uses to reveal himself, we can learn what he wants us to know about him. Although he is explained throughout this book, in this chapter we shall address a few problems that may hinder some people from believing in the biblical God of love.

FIVE PROBLEMS HINDERING FAITH IN GOD

(1) EXCLUSIVITY

One problem some have with God is his exclusiveness. He claims to be the only God we are to worship, and Jesus, who is equal with God, is the only way to come to God (Isaiah 45:22; John 14:6; Acts 4:12). People say it is arrogant to say his way is the only right way, implying that all who do not believe in him are wrong. Jesus said we are to worship God only (Luke 4:8). From God's Ten

Commandments we are warned not to have idols; that is, no other gods are to be put before him (Exodus 20:1-4). The Bible says, "For all the gods of the peoples are idols, but the Lord made the heavens" (1 Chronicles 16:26). God claims to be the only God (Isaiah 45:5). Why does he? Jesus said it is because he is the only God (John 5:44; 17:3). He is the only existing reality without beginning or end (Isaiah 40:28; Psalm 90:2). He is the creator of all things, both visible and invisible, and the only author of life (Colossians 1:16; Genesis 2:7). People's imagined gods and false ideas about God, along with all created things, are lesser and temporary. Jesus said they are passing away (Matthew 5:18; Luke 21:33). As Creator, God is outside of space and time, separate from all material things, self-existing, and personal. The God of love hates idolatry because he knows that belief in other gods will lead away from true life, a life that is rich in goodness, peace, happiness, and love, a life that can only be found in him.

Other gods people choose for themselves often include objects that are created, such as the sun, moon, or stars. One of the most popular objects of worship is nature. Nature worshippers define their god as pantheistic. Pantheism means that god is everything, and everything is god. There are many views of this idea of god. A pantheistic god is not a personal being separate and distinct from all else but an energy that pervades all things. We ourselves are part of god. The goal is to experience peace and love through meditation on nature, thus becoming one with god and the world around us. One of the benefits of nature worship that some say they enjoy is freedom from the biblical God who is seen as controlling and mean. Another benefit of believing in a pantheistic god is that we, by using the god powers inherent within us, can overcome our problems by controlling our own destinies and creating our own reality. I'm sure many find this way of life fulfilling, but does the worship of nature, or any other god, really fulfill all that people are looking for and needing, or do they still feel something is missing?

Jesus, who was sent into our world by the God of love, offers an alternative. He said, "I am the way, and the truth, and the life." He said, "I came that you might have life, and have it abundantly" (John 14:6; 10:10). Of course, Jesus himself does not allow us to have a totally rosy picture of life in this world, for he reminds his followers that in this world we will also have times of suffering and pain (Mark 10:28-30). However, God's love, peace, and joy are always there, like rays of the sun breaking through the dark clouds, giving us light and warmth and life-sustaining energy to overcome the darkness.

In considering the best option for a God worth believing in, here are essential questions to ask. Do I have an accurate view of the God of the Bible? How do all the promises of the God of the Bible differ from the promises of the pantheistic god, or any other god? How does the God of the Bible, and various other gods, define what's wrong with the world and its people? Finally, what does the God of love and the other gods offer as the solution to what's wrong with the world and its people, what is their ultimate goal, and what makes you think your object of worship can make it happen?

(2) WE CANNOT SEE HIM

Here is another thing that may trouble people about the God of love. From the Bible we learn that God is Spirit and cannot be seen by humans (John 4:24; 1:18; 6:46). Some people say they can't believe in something they cannot see. One of Jesus' own disciples said he would not believe Jesus rose from the dead unless he could see him alive again (John 20:24-25). Jesus said, "Blessed are those who do not see, and yet believe" (John 20:29). We don't see the wind or gravity, but we believe in them because we can see or feel their effects. The Bible does say that God has appeared to people at various times (Genesis 18:1; Exodus 24:9-11). How is it possible that God cannot be seen but at times *is* seen? It is because God can take various forms to appear to people, but never is he seen as God the Father or in his infinite completeness as the triune God. We can see him by *"so far and no further"* kinds of appearances or by the effects of what he does.

(3) NATURE

Some may wonder how nature tells us things about God. If we believe that God is the Creator of all things, we can expect that many things we see in nature will reflect what its Maker is like. For example, one thing we learn from our study of nature is that all things are interdependent. This means nothing exists alone. Everything depends on something else for its continued existence, and everything gives to something else for its existence. From the Bible we learn that God, the Creator of this world, is also an interdependent being—Father, Son, and Holy Spirit. No one part of his triune nature exists apart from the others. In a sense, the world is a model of God's nature. God is an interdependent being in the dimension in which he dwells, so we in our earthly dimension are also interdependent beings who need each other.

Additionally, we need the earth. God created us to share its physicality (Genesis 2:7). Thus we need to care for the earth because humans and the earth contribute to the well-being of each other. God has made us one with nature, so much so that when humans are bodily resurrected at the end of this age, the earth will also be set free from its slavery to corruption and continue to be a habitation for our new bodily life (Romans 8:19-21; 2 Peter 3:13). When we look at the world around us and how much it meets human needs, it definitely seems to be made by someone who cared about the well-being of the life forms that live on the planet. It is as the Bible says: "He is the God who formed the earth and made it, he established it and did not create it a waste place, but formed it to be inhabited" (Isaiah 45:18).

(4) EXISTENCE OF EVIL

One of the biggest problems preventing people from believing in a God of love is the existence of evil. God has created all things for our enjoyment except one: we are not to be involved in anything evil (1 Timothy 4:4; Genesis 2:16-17). If God is love, how can he allow evil in the world? Why doesn't he do something to stop it? Why couldn't he have made a better world so we could live in peace and harmony without evil wrecking our lives and environment? Be assured of this, there is one thing the God of love is not: God is not evil and is not the source of evil (Psalm 5:4; James 1:13). As holy and good, he does not permit evil to become part of his nature. God knows there is potential for evil, and seemingly, evil only becomes a reality if admitted into existence. We could argue whether or not God, as a free-will being, can do evil, but in light of a scriptural understanding of God, even if he could do evil, he chooses not to because he knows that evil is the opposite of his goodness and is a destroyer of life and all that is good. God created us in his image, and we were made to be free-will beings. Evil is the one and only thing God warned the first humans to avoid. Could we say it is true that in our finiteness, because we are not God, we need to rely on God to tell us things that are outside of our experience? Therefore, there is need for faith and trust in God. There is need to do as he says, not because he is controlling but because he knows what is good, right, and best for us if we are to be able to develop our individual uniqueness. Perhaps, because of our finiteness, and knowing less than God, the first humans had a greater potential than God to yield to temptation and fall away into evil. Apparently so, for that is what happened when they failed to trust God and ignored his warning. By choosing to believe the reasoning of an evil tempter, humans opened the door to let evil into their lives and into the world.

Where did an evil tempter come from? According to scripture, besides humans, other kinds of living creatures were created— spiritual beings living in another dimension. God must have created them, or some of them, to also be free-will beings, and one or more of them apparently chose to do something they saw as a potential— namely, becoming independent of God. It is possible that such a being who had fallen into this evil became the tempter of humans. Jesus met this satanic being and was tempted to become independent of God, but unlike us, Jesus chose to stay true to God, resisted the temptation, and became the only human who has ever done it (Luke 4:1-13). It is known from scripture that God will at times allow evil to test our faith in him and our love for him (Job 2:1-10). God would rather we freely love him than to be created as a robot who is programmed by whatever data God puts into him or her.

There are those who do not understand that God is holy and untainted by evil. They choose to explain evil by inventing an eternal opposing god who is evil or by saying that the one and only God must have a dual nature and be both good and evil. When such a god is eternally both good and evil, one must choose what side of God to be on, and the conflict with evil will never end. This, however, is a false view of the God who makes himself known. The God of the Bible, although he did not cause the evil, nevertheless seemingly takes responsibility for evil. In his love, he has devised a plan to eliminate evil by creating a new world where all is forever restored to goodness (Acts 3:19-21). We may not know all the answers to how or why evil is here, but we do know what God intends for the future good of all.

Why does God not destroy all evil now? For now, God is curbing evil so that it is kept at bay. He does this by intervening in our world with acts of judgment to destroy certain evils (Genesis 18:20-21; 19:24-25), by involving us in doing good things that will help evil be overcome (Romans 12:17-21), and by establishing human government and law as an opposition to evil (Romans 13:1-5). We must, however, trust that God has good reasons for allowing evil to continue until his day of final judgment (Isaiah 13:9; 2 Peter 3:7). One reason is that humans, by their own evils, are the cause of much of the world's evil, and to destroy all evil now would mean destroying all people who are contributing to what's wrong with the world. Rather than do that, God's love is patient, and in his mercy, he delays his judgment of evil because he does not take pleasure in the death of the wicked, or of anyone, but wants all to come to repentance and live (Ezekiel 18:23, 32; 2 Peter 3:10).

The Bible is God's account of human history from beginning to end. It tells us his plan to rescue his world and us from evil, and it tells us what the God of love is doing to make it happen. Later, when Jesus comes to reign, he will rule with peace. God's ultimate plan is to create a new heaven and new earth where righteousness rules and evil is no more (2 Peter 3:10). If his plan is to create a new and evil-free world, he must also create a new kind of humanity to live in it, which he does (2 Corinthians 5:17; John 3:3-7). Those who belong to Christ will enjoy resurrection bodies that will no longer be infected by sin, and they will live in God's righteous kingdom forevermore.

(5) GOD'S WRATH

God's anger, wrath, and judgment is another reason for people to reject the God of the Bible. The wrathful side of God's character is not to be minimized. For example, his Word tells us, "A jealous and avenging God is the Lord; the Lord is avenging and wrathful. The Lord takes vengeance on his adversaries, and he reserves wrath for his enemies. The Lord is slow to anger and great in power, and the Lord will by no means leave the guilty unpunished" (Nahum 1:2-3). Statements and examples of his anger and wrath are expressed throughout the Old and New Testaments. In reading those things, we feel ourselves wincing and recoiling, thinking to ourselves, *How can God be a God of love and do such things?* I've felt that way.

In our human thinking, if a person is angry, full of wrath, and vengeful toward others, he or she is not loving. However, we need to stop and assess if we are gauging God's anger and wrath by how we see human anger wrongfully expressed. God does not express his anger the same way we do. In fact, God is against the ways we get angry and wrongly punish or hurt people. Our anger is not often controlled and justified as is his. The Bible says that "the anger of man does not achieve the righteousness of God" (James 1:20). God encourages us to put our damaging forms of anger away (Colossians 3:8). God knows we cannot prevent our becoming angry, but he says, "Be angry, and do not sin" (Ephesians 4:26). God is slow to anger. It is not something that suddenly comes upon him, causing him to "fly off the handle" so to speak. He is gracious in giving people warnings and time to change their hurtful ways. Daniel, a prophet of God, was himself suffering God's wrath against him and his people, but he justifies God's righteous anger and judgments because God's love, in the form of warnings, had gone unheeded by his people and had led to their increased wickedness (Daniel 9:4-14). To Daniel, God loves people by exercising judgment and justice so that, by removing evil conditions, good can survive. More about this will be shared in the next chapter on love and war.

ACCEPTANCE OF THE GOD OF LOVE

Many choose to believe in the God of the New Testament because he is a God of love who forgives unconditionally. They choose not to believe in the God of the Old Testament who they perceive as a judgmental and mean God who condemns and punishes people. In this way, they can accept the God who is good and do away with the other God. However, this view of the biblical God is difficult to sustain in view of the fact that God is the same in both testaments (Numbers 14:18; Deuteronomy 7:9-10; John 3:36; Hebrews 10:26-

31). How then are we to understand and accept a God of love who is also angry and wrathful? One answer we use to cover our problem with God is to try and explain and defend his anger by looking at the reasons he gives for it. Such an approach can be helpful, but I wonder if an understanding of God's anger might better be helped by giving an increased amount of focus on God's love.

God in the Old Testament is not only a righteous and just God who judges and sentences wicked people to death, he is also well known as a God who loves. Over and over, we see examples of God's compassion, long-suffering, gracious mercy, lovingkindness, and forgiveness. We live in a world where peace and goodness are threatened by evils of all kinds, where the wrongful ways humans treat other humans happen far too often. Seeing deeper into the love of God helps us understand the necessity of appropriate anger, wrath, judgment, and justice, and we realize love that is blind to justice and allows evil to continue is no love at all.

What would happen if we changed our approach to reading the Bible? Instead of letting ourselves be drawn to and disgusted by the anger and wrath of God, what if we approached our reading by letting ourselves be drawn to what it says about the God's love? To help us see the depth and frequency of God's love operating in the Old Testament, I have listed the following situations to look for in our reading.

1. In reading, notice many times and situations where God's lovingkindness is mentioned. For example, "The Lord is compassionate and gracious, slow to anger, and abounding in lovingkindness and truth, who keeps lovingkindness for thousands, who forgives iniquity, transgression, and sin" (Exodus 34:6-7). A few other places include 1 Kings 8:23; Psalm 136; 145:8-9, 17-20; 146:5-9; and Isaiah 54:7-10.

2. God's love occurs in many places where he shows favor to individuals and nations from all walks of life. For example, Hagar (Genesis 16:1-13); Lot (Genesis 19:12-16); Naaman (2 Kings 5:1-17); Rahab (Joshua 2:8-14); Ebed-melech (Jeremiah 39:15-18); Nineveh, a wicked city (Jonah 1:1-2; 3:1-10); sinners (Psalm 32:1-5).

3. We see God's love wherever he gives us laws to live by that lead to a good life. Many think Jesus is the one who taught us to love our neighbors as ourselves and to love our enemies. Actually, these are quotes by Jesus from God's laws in the Old Testament (Leviticus 19:17-18; Proverbs 25:21-22). God's social laws were laws on how to treat others with love, fairness, and righteousness (Leviticus 19:10, 15, 32-34; Deuteronomy 15:7-11). How would our world be different if we all lived by his Ten Commandments (Exodus 20:1-17; Deuteronomy 5:7-21)?

4. We see God's love in all the places where he prophecies and promises to give all peoples a Savior who will do away with evil and rule the world with peace and righteousness. For example, Genesis 3:15; 12:1-3; Isaiah 9:6-7; 53:4-6; Daniel 7:13-14; Zechariah 14:1-9. The New Testament records the fulfillment of these promises.

5. We see God's love throughout the Bible whenever he works to ensure the coming of his promised Messiah. God acts against enemies who would destroy Israel and the genealogical lineage that would prevent the Christ from being born. For example, the pharaoh of Egypt ordered the death of all Israelite baby boys so as to keep Israel from growing in numbers and to keep their nation in slavery. Pharaoh tried to stop Moses from leading the people out of slavery and into God's Promised Land, the birthplace of Christ (Exodus 1:15-22; Micah 5:2). In the days following Babylonian captivity, when under Persian rule, it was decreed that the Jewish people were to be annihilated. Queen Esther helped to save them (Esther 3:13; 7:1-7). Cyrus, founder of the Persian Empire, was used by God to allow captured Jews to go back to their destroyed homeland and rebuild their nation (Isaiah 44:24-28; 45:1, 13). Herod, King in Israel, ordered all baby boys in Bethlehem to be killed hoping to stop the Christ from becoming king. But the God who loves the world saw to it that nothing would stop the Savior from being born as he promised (Matthew 2:1-8, 16).

CHAPTER 3: UNDERSTANDING THE GOD OF LOVE

6. We see God's love in all the situations where he warns people of their wicked ways, seeking their repentance so they will not destroy people and the good life God wants for all (Genesis 19:12-16; Jeremiah 44:2-6). God is not being mean to warn people any more than we are sometimes warned of a storm that is coming. The warning is because there is real danger, and we could lose our lives. It would be cruel to know about the storm and not warn people. In the beginning, God warned the first man and woman, pointing out to them that all of creation was for their enjoyment and that nothing was forbidden to them, except one thing. The one thing was to fail to heed his warning, for if they did, it would allow evil into the world, resulting in its destructive ways. Evil is the opposite of what God is like, and it destroys all that is good. God continues to give warnings to all, along with adequate time to repent and change (Ezekiel 18:23, 32; Mark 1:14-15; Luke 13:1-5).

7. We see God's love when he must judge and destroy those who have not heeded his gracious warnings—those whose wickedness has gone beyond remedy (Proverbs 29:1; 2 Chronicles 36:15-16). God does this to protect and free those who are victims suffering injustice at the hands of wrongdoers.

8. We see God's love in all the places where God makes merciful provision for the forgiveness of people's wrongs so they can be freed from guilt and condemnation and live in God's good favor. God makes provision for people to receive his forgiveness (Leviticus 5:5-10; Psalm 130:3-4; Isaiah 43:25; Daniel 9:9).

9. We see God's love in the places where his grief, sadness, and sorrow are expressed concerning people he must judge and discipline or destroy. Many do not see this tender side of God's nature. For example, when Jesus, representing the true likeness of God (Hebrews 1:3), noticed how death caused pain and suffering in people, he wept (John 11:33-36). We see his sorrow again near the end of Jesus' life,

59

when he approached the city of Jerusalem. He had tried to tell the people and their religious leaders that he was sent by God to save and heal them, but most mocked him, doubted him, and did not believe what he was saying. As he approached the city that was about to kill him, he wept, knowing that God would judge them, many would die, and their city would be destroyed (Luke 19:41-44).

There is an interesting Bible passage in the book of Proverbs, showing something of the softness of God's heart. If God sees us rejoicing when our enemies fall or stumble, he will be displeased and may then turn his anger away from our enemies (Proverbs 24:17-18). Of course, there is a place for rejoicing when God relieves us of those who are oppressing us (Proverbs 11:10), but still, our attitude and lifestyle toward our enemies is to treat them as God does—to love them and do good to them (Job 31:29-30; Psalm 35:12-14; Matthew 5:44-48; Romans 12:19-21). If they are loved, it may change them as it has us. However, God's heart grieves the works of evil. He has a deep sorrow over what those who reject him are doing and how it's hurting themselves and others (Genesis 6:5-6). There comes a time when God knows that to preserve goodness and protect others, it is time to exercise his justice and rid the world of people determined to reject God and remain in their wicked lifestyles. Knowing that the evil will not go away and "innocent" people are suffering, he destroys the evils that destroy his world and its people.

I do not want to minimize the terrible evils in this world that cause unimaginable suffering and pain. We can't bear to see or even think about such awful and tortuous things. I empathize with people who are unable to accept any word about God and God's love. Understandably, many are in a position to ask how a God of love can allow such things to go on. I have no final answers to all of the problems involving God and the existence of evil. But I do know of things I experience in my own life when it comes to judging others. For one thing, I can make no judgments about God's handling of evil, for I have found that I am not even capable of accurately judging people, or even myself. We humans judge people, but we do not know enough to make an accurate or righteous judgment about who they really are or why they do what they do. As best we can, we judge with limited knowledge. We may get some things right, but not everything. The more we know, the better we can adjust our judgments to fit the facts.

I see God the same way. I do not know enough to judge him rightly. Judgment is an interesting thing. There are always aspects in a person and in a situation that we do not see, unknowns that would make accurate judgment difficult. Plus, every person and situation in some way differs from others, making it necessary to render a different judgment in each and every case. A God who knows all is capable of total righteous judgment, and we are not. Because God says so about himself, I choose to accept God as love and goodness and also as a punisher of evil (Exodus 34:5-7). I may never understand some things about God's handling of evil, but one thing I do know is that God says he loves us and is not wishing that any person dies. He wants to see all repent and learn to trust him, and in the end, he saves all who want to be saved and creates a new heaven and earth for their dwelling place—a place where evil no longer exists.

Thus I try to live in this world of good and evil as he says to live, with faith, hope, and love. I believe him when he says that good triumphs over evil, so with his help to change me, I try to practice his kind of goodness. I also believe it when he says we have the sentence of death within us so that we would not trust in ourselves but in God who raises the dead. The evidence I find in history concerning the resurrection of Christ Jesus gives me assurance that God can and will fulfill all the promises he gives us.

I feel sorry for people in this world who believe only in themselves and certain philosophies they have come to accept. I give them credit for wanting to change the world, for like all of us, they too have a sense of good and evil, right and wrong. They obviously see some evils that need changing, and we as humans would do well to listen to each other. Nevertheless, to make good changes requires that we are able to distinguish between good and evil ways to make those changes. I believe God is the ultimate source of knowing what is good and what is evil, and he can give us wisdom to know the difference. Otherwise, we end up taking matters into our own hands, and the ways we use to bring about change end up destroying the very life we want to see happen.

I have been taking a college course in quantum physics from a professor at one of our universities. She does a great job of relating what science is learning about the tiny invisible parts of matter that make up the building blocks of our world. Many today think that we humans can create our own reality and destiny. What we learn through experiments in quantum science is that we can affect the direction of the quantum world by doing things we want to see happen, but when we do, we end up, in some way, changing the systems that make that world what it is designed to be. In other words, by trying to be our own god, we can end up destroying ourselves. That is what evil does. Like in quantum world experiments, we have not yet learned how to affect change without possibly destroying the world we are trying to change.

CONCLUSION

God is love, but he is also many other things. For example, he is a God of holiness and justice and judgment and anger and wrath and putting people to death—and so forth. These are things people have a hard time equating with a God of love. Without a full understanding of God or things like the meaning of death, who are we to criticize God? Who are we to blame God for the way things are? Who are we to say what he should or should not do? Who are we to say he doesn't care about me or listen to me? When we have such thoughts and attitudes toward God, we are doing what the evil tempter wants us to do. We are putting ourselves above God. We are trying to dictate to him what we think he ought to be and do. We are agreeing with those who have seen the truth that we want to make God into our image rather than let him make us into his image. Am I that grand that I want God to be like me? Am I somebody worth being like, and God is not?

We so easily focus on the negative. We focus on the things about God we don't agree with. God wants us to understand a bigger picture of who he truly is and not fix our sights on those attributes that we think put him beneath us. God wants us to see how great is his love for us, but the evil one would block out the good so that we cannot see it. Jesus once said that he did not come to judge us but to save us (John 12:47). Let us stop judging God and let him save us. Let us not be God, but let us be who we are—people in need of someone to save us from who are so that we can be someone who is truly good and loving and wise and kind, like God. Let us stop demeaning him or others as if we are the one who people ought to be following. Perhaps I am now preaching to myself. If so, I deserve it, for I loathe that side of myself that I would rather not see. I need to side with the Apostle Paul: "Who will free me from the body of this death?" (Romans 7:24).

I am humbled, and I pray, *Lord, save me. Let me see how much you love me and this world you have created. Let your love be my focus so that I can see how all you do is done in love. Let me see that you really are working to restore all things and that it is your love that will conquer all. It is your love we need. It is your love that brings us back to you. It is your love that changes us. It is your love that takes a world gone astray and recreates it so you can do again what you did in the beginning when you looked at what you made, and "saw that it was good"* (Genesis 1:9, 18, 25), *"very good"* (Genesis 1:31). *Praise be to the God of love who does not forsake his creation but is faithful to redeem it and free it from its corruption so it shall be good again. As one of your 2 Corinthians 5:17 new creations in Christ, I can't wait to see it and experience its beauty. You are truly the God of love who makes all things new and right* (Revelation 21:1-5).

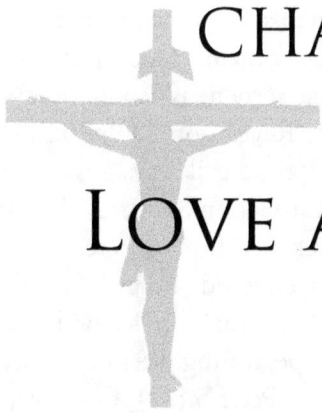

CHAPTER 4

LOVE AND WAR

War seems like a strange thing to include in a book about love. But isn't it true that war is most likely fought over things we love? Although those things can be good things, like freedom, the problem is that the things we love and fight for are not always things that are good for us, nor things worth loving. They are often things we lust after—things we don't have but want—so we go to war to get them (James 4:1-4). Nations will go to war to fulfill their lust for power, supremacy, increased territory, revenge, or wealth, or to spread their ideologies, philosophies, values, or religion. Most often, one side is the aggressor, out to get from others the things they want, while the opposing side is only fighting in self-defense to protect themselves from suffering losses, enslavement, or being killed. War does not only exist between nations, but there is fighting between people in families and communities for similar reasons—to gain something they want. It seems there is always war, or threats of war, going on somewhere in the world.

But there is a greater war going on in the world, perhaps the only one that actually matters. It is the war between good and evil. It is a war that causes the wars described above. It is a spiritual warfare. Not only do each of us face inner battles between good and evil, but at the level of family and community, evil creates conflicts that cause us to be against one another—dividing us, even destroying many in its wake. The fact is, spiritual warfare has existed from the very beginning of God's creation. The first man and woman were engaged in a spiritual war involving themselves, a loving God, and an evil serpent. Near the end of the Bible, that serpent is represented as a dragon and is called the devil and Satan (Revelation 12:9; 20:2). The serpent is a clever and convincing liar whose evil ways ensnare and enslave people in destructiveness and death (John 8:44). God created everything good, and evil tries to wreck it. Humans, created with freedom of will, are given a choice between good and evil, and God, in his goodness and love, warns them where their choice will lead— either to life or to death. Today, as in the beginning, we find ourselves in the same war between good and evil (1 Peter 5:8-9). Our struggle is over which one will be our master (1 John 3:10-12; Genesis 4:6-7).

Whether we agree with a biblical worldview or not, the reality is that there is good and evil in the world. Evil can be very deceptive because it can appear to be good. It seems the Bible is right when it says that evil can appear as an angel of light, deceptively disguised by making things seem decent, civil, right, and good (2 Corinthians 11:14-15). A proverb says, "There is a way which seems right to a man, but its end is the way of death" (Proverbs 14:12). Although humans have an inborn sense that right and wrong exists, they cannot always agree on what it is, for they can call good "evil" and evil "good" (Isaiah 5:20-21). This is why there needs to be a clear way to know what is right and what is wrong, what is good and what is evil. Who better to determine what is right and wrong than a holy God who is wholly righteous, allowing no evil in his being or kingdom. God's character defines what is right and good, and he lets us know by giving us a written Word that includes things like the Ten Commandments and his laws of love.

Most people want there to be love, kindness, forgiveness, goodness, and peace. A biblical psalm writer said, "Too long has my soul had its dwelling with those who hate peace. I am for peace, but when I speak, they are for war" (Psalm 120:6-7). Sadly, evils within us and around us prevent us from enjoying any permanent peace. Yet, in God and his Messiah, there is hope for everlasting victory over evil, and there is hope for everlasting peace (Isaiah 2:4; 9:6-7; Zechariah 9:9-10). In our human inability to overcome such powerful forces of evil, we need someone who is for us and who will fight for us. Who will it be? Every story and event throughout the entire Bible is about the ongoing war between good and evil. To win the battle between good and evil, we must all yield to a good and righteous Warrior who is able to lead with a plan and empower us to victory.

GOD IS A WARRIOR

The first mention of God as a warrior came after the Lord, in an act of love, saved those he had chosen to become a nation. He saved them from the Egyptian army at the Red Sea. Moses wrote a song in which he said of God, "The LORD is a warrior; the LORD is his name" (Exodus 15:3). Many years later, the prophet Isaiah recorded, "The LORD will go forth like a warrior, He will arouse *His* zeal like a man of war. He will utter a shout, yes, He will raise a war cry. He will prevail against his enemies" (Isaiah 42:13). Another prophet, in the midst of threats to his people's well-being, gives them hope with these words: "The LORD your God is in your midst, a victorious warrior. He will exult over you with joy, He will be quiet in his love, He will rejoice over you with shouts of joy" (Zephaniah 3:17).

The God of the Bible, who owns numerous names and character traits, is a warrior. He is often called "The Lord of hosts"—that is, "Lord of armies." There apparently also existed a book called the "Book of the Wars of the Lord" (Numbers 21:14). Who does God war against, and who does he go to war for? God is a warrior against Satan and against people who willfully engage in destructive and wrongful behaviors, ruining themselves and the world around them. God is a warrior on behalf of those who trust him (Exodus 14:13-14; Deuteronomy 20:2-4) and are called to be coworkers with him in his salvation plan (Ephesians 2:10; 1 Corinthians 15:58). Those who are God's people are not on their own in their spiritual warfare, for God is with them and gives them victory (Psalm 44:1-8; Isaiah 41:10-12).

A Difference between Holy War and God's War

You may have heard the term *holy war* used by various religious groups to say that they are fighting a war on behalf of their god. Unfortunately, Christians, among others, are guilty of fighting holy wars, and in doing so, do they not fail to understand the biblical God and his ways? There is a distinction between *holy wars* and *God's wars*. *Holy wars* are wars initiated and fought by humans on behalf of their god or gods, and *God's wars* are wars initiated and fought by God on behalf of his people. *Holy wars* are fought by humans who wrongly seek to have their desires met, using their god or gods as a reason to justify their actions. In *God's wars*, it is not the people who go to war to achieve God's will; rather, God goes to war to accomplish his own righteous objectives. *Holy wars* originate from humans who do not have a specific and proven word from the one and only God of the Bible to fight the wars. *God's wars* originate with the one and only God, and those who join him in battle have a definite indication— that is, his personal contact or miraculous signs proving he is in charge and has enlisted them to join him.

Often, in *God's wars*, the people do not have to do much fighting, for God fights for them, as he did in Egypt. *God's wars* are fought over the issue of good versus evil. He fights to bring about what is good, to destroy what is evil, to protect people from evil's corruption and afflictions, and to work toward the completion of his plan to bring about a new and evil-free world. God's plan will be fulfilled and completed by his promised Messiah. The Messiah's method of war in these present days involves weapons of grace, love, and truth, rather than the methods of *God's wars* as previously fought in Old Testament days. *Holy wars* are usually fought to force others into submission to one's own ways of life. Today, *God's wars* are fought through a spiritual warfare involving the Messiah's death and resurrection, and it changes people's hearts into love and peace as the way to win the war against evil. A better understanding of God's warfare and God's purposes, past, present, and future, becomes clearer as one more closely examines the Old and New Testaments of the Bible.

GOD'S CHARACTER AND PURPOSE

Before examining Old Testament wars, we need to have a clearer understanding of God's holy nature as it relates to his wars. When God created the heavens, the earth, people, and life, he saw all he had made, and it was very good (Genesis 1:31). It can't be said that something is good unless there is also something that is not good. God knows there is something potentially not good called *evil* that ruins and destroys what is good. Although God is good and no evil dwells in him (Psalm 5:4), evil entered God's good world through humans who chose to allow an evil influence and person into their lives and thereby into the world. What does God do about this cancer that corrupts, eats up, and ruins his good world? Does he abandon everything to an inevitable end of destruction? No! He loves the world and does something about it (John 3:16). He has a plan to redeem his world—that is, to restore it to goodness. He has been working his plan from the beginning of its fall into evil hands, and he continues to work his plan in every present moment until it is successfully completed in the end. We do not know all the details of his plan, nor do we always understand why he does what he does; we are only asked to trust his wisdom, goodness, and power to bring about his promises.

The Bible is God's written record of what he has been doing, what he is doing, and what he will do to bring about a warless world. God can choose to change things from the way they are to the way he wants them to be. We humans are created in his image, and one thing this means is that we too have a mind. Our lives do not have to stay the same because we also have a mind that can choose to change things. The difference between God and us is that we do not have the same power to change things that he has. God is sovereign over all, and we are not. Therefore, our choices cannot overrule his choices but must operate within the good, loving, wise, reasonable, and righteous boundaries that he sets. We humans can choose what will be sovereign over us. Will we yield to good or evil? That choice determines our end—whether life or death.

Because God's plan is to restore his world to goodness, he must not allow evil to continue to ruin it. He must have a way to eliminate evil, including a way for humans to be rid of evil, so that God and humans can work together toward the goal of restoring all things to what is good. Humans have choices to make, but the evil that has gotten into us can be too powerful for us to overcome. We find ourselves powerless to choose consistently what is right and good, and even if we could, the evil that is in the world around us does not let our choices ultimately succeed. Thankfully, because God loves us, he includes in his plan a way to help us be able to choose the same things he chooses. He does this by drawing us to himself and providing a way for our hearts to be changed, thus allowing us to freely choose his ways and work together with him to change ourselves and the world into the kind of world he intends.

Sadly, many continue to resist his plan, insisting on their own way. They lack the wisdom to see the future results of their choices. Also, the evil in them, the kind of evil that acts out in wicked behavior and the kind that appears civil, good, and right, continues to contribute to the ruin of the world, themselves, and other humans. When they become hardened against God to a point beyond remedy, and his love is ultimately rejected, the evils through them continue to grow. Therefore, God is unapologetic and honest in revealing two aspects of his nature that are needed to provide victory over evil, both for him and for us. Those two aspects are his love and his justice. He clearly reveals in his written Word that he is a God who is compassionate and gracious, slow to anger, abounding in lovingkindness and truth, who forgives iniquity, transgression and sin; but also, he is a God who will not leave the guilty unpunished and who will destroy those who hate him (Exodus 34:6-7; Deuteronomy 7:9-10). His Word says, "Let God arise, let his enemies be scattered, and let those who hate him flee before him" (Psalm 68:1). In God's warfare to overcome evil, his love forgives and changes people into doers of good, while his justice deals with people who keep resisting his love and who continue to threaten his plan to redeem and restore his world. Evil cannot be overcome by those who insist on doing it their own way. Rather, evil is overcome through God-motivated acts of love and doing good (Romans 12:14-21). If evildoers are engaged in destroying what is good, God can choose to step in and stop the ruin of that good, though it may not happen as soon as we would like.

As a warrior, God fights for his people and enlists them to cooperate with him in the kind of warfare that results in goodness.

The following stories demonstrate both his love and justice as he works his plan to restore the world (Acts 3:17-26). I have chosen examples of God's love and justice from four biblical periods of history: the conquest of the Canaanites in the book of Joshua; the period of the judges; the era of Israel's kings and prophets; and the times of Christ Jesus. Some people tend to see God in the Old Testament as legalistic, judgmental, and mean. Do we have a view of God that is too narrow to see throughout the Bible the extent of his love, patience, and forgiveness? Do we truly understand the purpose for his laws and why he does what he does? Furthermore, have we fully taken into account the severity of the evils and wickedness in this world when those evils go unchecked? Finally, have we observed God's grieving heart over not wanting anyone to perish and over having to punish those who will not change? The goal in this chapter is to see more of the loving side of God and his purposes as we examine a few examples of God's wars in these four areas of biblical history.

CONQUEST OF THE CANAANITES

We begin with a brief background of Canaan. Noah, who built an ark to survive a flood, had a grandson named Canaan (Genesis 9:18-19). Noah cursed Canaan, who later proved to exceed the immoral ways of his father, Ham. The curse prophesied that Canaan would one day be servant to his brothers, Shem and Japheth (Genesis 9:25-26). This prophesy was fulfilled through a man named Abram, a descendant of Shem (Genesis 11:10-27). Abram was called by God to leave his country and go to a land God would show him (Genesis 12:1). That land, made up of many tribes that were descendants of Noah's grandson, turned out to be the future land called Canaan (Genesis 10:15-19). Abram was given three promises from God. First, he was promised that God would make from him a great nation (Genesis 12:2). That nation was Israel. Second, God promised Abram that his nation would inherit the land God had shown him (Genesis 15:17-21; 17:7-8). The conquest of the Canaanites fulfilled that promise. Third, God promised that the whole world would be blessed in Abram through his seed (Genesis 12:3; 22:18). The blessing of the whole world was, and will be, ultimately fulfilled through Abraham's promised son and future descendant, Jesus Christ (Genesis 22:15-18; Galatians 3:8-9, 16). Abraham's offspring will be the Savior of the world and the hope of all mankind.[6]

God wants to create a world that blesses people, not a world that is destroyed by people with wicked intentions and actions. Such sinful mindsets and behaviors in people destroy life, but God's Spirit in people gives life. That's why God created a people who would love and follow him by practicing his loving ways. This, however, takes growing in that love and fighting the kind of warfare that overcomes evil. The conquest of Canaan is an example of taking people who are destroying people's lives and replacing them with a nation that blesses people with God's love and goodness. The nature of Canaanite wickedness is defined in Leviticus 18, and in that chapter the Israelites are admonished not to practice any of those kinds of behaviors.

An early example of Canaanite evil occurred in the days of Abraham. The history of Sodom was to serve as an example and warning to the future Canaanite peoples, and others, that God cannot allow wickedness of this extent to destroy his plan to bless the world (2 Peter 2:6). It was known that "the men of Sodom were wicked exceedingly and sinners against the Lord" (Genesis 13:13; 18:20). One day two men from God appeared to Abraham and said they were going to Sodom to assess the evils being reported and, depending on the severity, would destroy the city. Abraham appealed to God not to destroy the city if at least ten righteous people lived there, for he could not believe God would destroy the righteous along with the wicked (Genesis 18:22-25).

When the two men got to Sodom, Abraham's nephew, Lot, would not let the men stay anywhere but in his home, for he knew it was not safe. Lot knew that the people rebelled against authority and

---

6. Abram's name, *exalted father*, was later changed by God to Abraham, *father of a multitude* (Genesis 17:5). God made a covenant with him, promising that he would become the father of many nations and that he would have a son through whom the Messiah would ultimately come, through whom all nations would be blessed (Genesis 17-18; Galatians 3:6-29).

were lawless, and it troubled his heart that they were so immoral and violent. Sure enough, people of the city surrounded Lot's house and demanded that the two men be sent out so they could abuse them sexually and violently. When Lot pleaded with them not to do this, they accused Lot of judging them, and they began to break down his door. By the power of God, the two men caused them to be blinded, and in the morning, because of the compassion of God, they took Lot and his family out of there before the city was destroyed with fire and brimstone (Genesis 19:15-25).

God shows his love to the righteous, but punishment comes to the wicked who refuse to repent and turn from their evil ways. The God of love would rather save and bless than destroy, but there comes a time when people's wickedness is beyond remedy (Proverbs 6:12-15; 29:1; Romans 1:28-32). Centuries later, the Canaanites were widely known for their ungodly abominations. God's war against them was a judgment against evil that was beyond remedy for those who had so hardened their hearts that they refused to repent.

The Israelites eventually take over the Canaanites' land. Unlike Canaanite evil and harmful ways of living, the Israelites were to bless people by loving their neighbor as God commanded. God's people were to be holy as he is holy, practicing his laws of love. Those laws included the following:

- When you harvest your crops, leave some for the poor and needy.
- Be good and kind to the stranger in your midst.
- Don't steal nor deal falsely nor lie to one another.
- Care for the deaf and the blind.
- Treat each other fairly, and don't withhold wages from your workers.
- Don't hate your fellow countrymen in your heart; don't take revenge or bear a grudge against him or her.
- Don't engage in sexual immorality of any kind, such as intercourse with an animal or with another man's wife.
- Respect and honor the elderly.

- Do not do wrong to foreigners who live among you.
- Do not be like the Canaanites who sacrifice their children in the fire to their god.

The Israelites are to live in the ways of love that God had commanded (see Leviticus 18-20). They are to keep wickedness out of their personal lives, families, communities, and nation. When they fail, as we all do, there is provision for restoration through forgiveness. They are to love as God has loved them. They are to overcome evil by doing good.

God's love for the Canaanites gave them ample time to repent of their wickedness and turn to him and his good way of life. In fact, God's love is exhibited in telling Abraham that he would not allow his nation to conquer the Canaanites and possess their land until the iniquity of the Canaanite nation, represented by a people called the Amorites, was complete (Genesis 15:12-16). God's lovingkindness, patience, and slowness to anger gives the Canaanites well over four hundred years of grace to take advantage of God's warnings and repent, turn from their wrongdoings, and do as Abraham did—be made righteous by faith in God (Genesis 15:6).

God's wars in Canaan were to fulfill his own righteous purposes. He let his people Israel know that his war against Canaan had nothing to do with them or how righteous they might think they are. In fact, he told them, "You are a stubborn people," but because of the wickedness of these nations, God is driving them out before you (Deuteronomy 9:1-6). The job of God's people was to submit to God's orders, not fear the overwhelming strength of their enemies, and trust God to give them the victory. Israel is joining God in his fight against evil and assisting him in the bringing about of a better world. God does the fighting and directs his people on what he wants them to do. He is the one in charge, not them. All credit for the victories goes to their Lord God.

Before moving on to the period of the judges, here are two examples of God's war in the conquest of Canaan, demonstrating how he fights for his people while at the same time loving and saving people who turn to him.

In the battle against Jericho, God fights for his people by having them march around the fortified city seven times, blow their trumpets, and shout, and the walls would fall down (Joshua 6:15-21). Before that victory, the Canaanite people of Jericho had opportunity to repent and experience God's salvation. We know this through the story of a woman, a harlot named Rahab. She and her family were saved because she did believe in the God of the Israelites. Her faith in God caused her to hide Israelite spies who had come there earlier to check things out. She asked them to save her and the life of her family. What she knew about their God was also the same information the other people knew, and they could have repented as she did but did not. She and the people heard about how the God of Israel dried up the Red Sea to enable his people to escape from Egypt and how he destroyed the Egyptian army, and they knew that this God had defeated two Amorite kings on the other side of the Jordan River. Here are her words to the spies who visited her: "I know that the Lord has given you this land." She admitted that her people were afraid because they knew that "the Lord your God, He is the God in heaven above and on earth beneath" (Joshua 2:1-14). Yet she submitted her life to God, and they did not. Because of her faith, when Jericho and its people were destroyed, she and her family were rescued (Joshua 6:16-17; Hebrews 11:31). Rahab is mentioned as one of the persons in the genealogy of Christ (Matthew 1:5). She is an example of God's compassion, forgiveness, and love, and how God wants to bless persons from every nation as he promised Abraham.

A second example of God's wars in Canaan involves the Canaanite nation of Gibeon, a people greatly respected for their military power. Knowing their lives were in trouble, they lied to Israel and craftily fooled Israel into sparing them. Israel made a covenant of peace with them, and Gibeon promised to be their servants. Later, when five Amorite kings found out Gibeon had betrayed them and made peace with Israel, they brought their five armies to destroy them. Knowing they could not defeat five armies, Gibeon appealed to Israel to save them (Joshua 9:3-10:14). In spite of the Gibeonite lies and deceptions and in spite of Israel's failure to check with God on what to do with Gibeon, God graciously spared the Gibeonites because of their faith in his power. God led Israel to their rescue, battled these five armies, and once again fought for his people, including the Gibeonites whom he once intended to destroy. He hurled huge hailstones, killing more soldiers in the enemy Amorite armies than Israel did with their swords (Joshua 10:11).

What actually happened with God's wars in Canaan? In keeping with his revelation that he was a God of love and a God of justice who punishes evil (Exodus 34:6-7), God justly condemned the wicked and, as promised, gave their land to Israel (Deuteronomy 7:1-26). Throughout the biblical book of Joshua, the destruction of Canaan was God's war. God was the one who dried up the Jordan River so his people could cross into Canaan. God was the one who fought for his people with miracles and directions on when and how to defeat their enemies. Canaan was divided among the tribes of Israel, and they lived peacefully in the land. Joshua, God's chosen military and spiritual leader, gathered the people together before he died and told them that God had fulfilled what he promised to Abraham by giving the land of Canaan to his descendants (Joshua 23:14). Joshua also warned them to remain separate from the Canaanite people who were still living in the land. They were to continue driving them out so as not to follow them in their ungodly and wicked ways. If they failed in this and allowed the Canaanite ways to corrupt them, God would drive Israel out of the land just as he did the Canaanites (Joshua 23:15-16). Joshua encouraged them to continue serving God, and the people committed themselves to doing so (Joshua 24:14-18). In the end, God's command to destroy the wicked people of the land turned out not to be a total or complete destruction; yet, it was enough to make the Canaanite nations back down, allowing God's people to take possession of the land.

In some of the Canaanite battles, according to God's instructions, every person was killed, but this was not the case for all of the cities and tribes in Canaan. There were three reasons for this. First, in some cases the people refused to obey God's command to destroy them (Joshua 16:10, 17:12-13; Judges 1:21, 27-35). This would later lead to Israel's downfall. Second, the prophecy that Canaan would become servant to his brothers was fulfilled (Genesis 9:24-26). Third, God left many Canaanite people alive to test the hearts of his people to see if they would fight the spiritual battles necessary to follow God and not yield to Canaanite gods and ways (Judges 2:20-23).

Something I've noticed about God all through the Bible is how much love he has for all people, no matter what their situation. He does not want anyone to die, for he takes no pleasure in the death of anyone, including the wicked. He wants all of us to come to repentance and live (Ezekiel 18:23, 32; John 3:16; 2 Peter 3:9). Once on God's side, he protects those who belong to him with his presence and words of guidance so that evil no longer has power to ultimately destroy them. God is the all-powerful warrior who protects his people against the evils that are constantly attacking them, and the last enemy he will destroy on their behalf, and ours, is death (1 Corinthians 15:26). Even in our sufferings from the evils of this world, God is faithful to be with us and not forsake us. Fear no evil, guard the knowledge of his presence, and keep listening to his Word and doing what he says, for he is with us no matter what we are going through. His salvation and future good certainly awaits those who trust in him (Psalm 23).

THE PERIOD OF THE JUDGES

After Joshua died, for a brief time, the Israelites continued to assist God in driving out the Canaanites (Judges 1:1-4). But it wasn't long before the people failed to heed God's warnings and began to mix with the Canaanites. They started following their practices and chose to worship their gods (Judges 2:1-3, 11-15). The period of the Judges was a continuous cycle of falling away from God, suffering the consequences of affliction and oppression by the Canaanites, crying out to God for help, and God raising up individuals to save them and to lead them back to him. Persons God raised up to deliver his people were called judges (Judges 2:16-18). Through these judges, God miraculously fought on behalf of his people, showing them there was no God like him. But after they were delivered, they were soon back to the ways of false gods and practicing the evils of the people around them who worshiped those gods. In those days, everyone did what was right in his or her own eyes—but not God's eyes (Judges 17:6; 21:25).

During this time, God continued his God wars, demonstrating again that he was a God who loved them and who would fight on their behalf. He gave them victory over their enemies in miraculous ways so that they would know and trust him rather than trust in themselves or other powers to save them. For example, at a time when his people were facing sure defeat from armies of about 135,000 soldiers (Judges 8:10), God called a man named Gideon to fight them but to reduce his army from 32,000 down to 300 (Judges 7:1-8). God did not want the people to think they could defeat Canaanite evil by their own human strength, which never works, but to trust in his love and power to overcome evil's threats. No matter how things look, his people must trust the God who loves them and will fight for them. Gideon was afraid, but God convinced him that he would be with him, told him what to do, confused the enemy, and gave him the victory.

God's wars continued through many other judges—for example, a man named Samson (Judges 13-16). God gave him super-human strength to defeat the enemies. The last of the judges was a God-appointed man named Samuel. In his days of leadership, Canaanites known as Philistines afflicted the ungodly Israelites. Samuel called the people to repent of their evil ways and come back to God, and when they did, God fought for them and helped Israel defeat the Philistines by a miraculous thundering from heaven (1 Samuel 7:1-14).

God's love is continually demonstrated in the time of the judges. Even though there was no king in Israel and the people kept going away from him and doing what was right in their own eyes, every time they cried out to him, he would overlook their evils and give them help (for example, see Judges 3:7-11; 6:1-16). Jesus, who is the exact representation of what God is like, taught the same thing in his day. He taught that when our brother sins against us, even up to seventy times seven, and comes to us with a repentant heart, we are to forgive (Matthew 18:21-22; Luke 17:3-4).

God's love in the days of the judges was also operating through his people in the biblical book of Ruth. Even though the Israelite culture as a whole was continually going away from God, there were those few who were faithful. The story of Ruth is a story that demonstrates God working through his faithful people to reach out in love to others, helping those from other cultures who do not know

God to come to know and love him. Such was the case with Ruth, and like Rahab, she became a solid believer who God worked through to keep the genealogy of his promised Messiah from being broken. The evil one would like nothing better than to prevent God's Messiah from coming into the world, but God will not let that happen. Many persons mentioned in the book of Ruth were believers who kept the Messianic hopes alive, not only for Israel but for the good of the whole world.

THE ERA OF ISRAEL'S KINGS AND PROPHETS

Following the period of the judges, the people wanted kings to reign over Israel and to be their saviors. In a sense, by doing this, they were rejecting God as their king and protector, but God gave them their wish (1 Samuel 8:4-22). During this period, after their third king, Israel was divided into two kingdoms—Israel to the north and Judah to the south. It was a time of good kings who did right in the sight of the Lord and also a time of evil kings who did wrong. Both kingdoms of Israel faced enemies who sought their destruction, and again, there were accounts of God's wars to help them. One story tells of an army over 185,000 who came against the Israelites, and God rescued his people by sending an angel to kill them (2 Kings 19:32-35). Again, the Israelites witnessed the power and love of God who fought on their behalf. He proved to them and other nations that he was the only true God worth loving (for example, 1 Samuel 5:2-7; 1 Kings 18:20-39). They had no excuse for trusting and serving other gods in place of the God of Abraham, their founding father.

Unfortunately, God's people, chosen to serve him as representatives of his love and righteousness, eventually fell away, and God punished them by removing them from their promised land of Canaan. The Israelites, with the exception of a few, no longer listened to God and obeyed his word, which as a nation they previously had agreed to do. They dedicated objects in God's temple to false gods, building altars to Baal and a statue of a female deity for their worship. Idolatrous priests led in the worship of these gods and of the starry host of heaven. Cult prostitutes performed immoral acts in the house of the Lord. People were sacrificing their children in the fires of the god Molech. They dedicated their horses and chariots to other gods and countries. The people were taxed and the money given to foreign nations to come and fight their enemies. Forbidden spiritists, mediums, and witchcraft practitioners, along with many idols, were consulted by people throughout the land. Jerusalem was filled with violence, and many innocent people were being killed (see 2 Kings 22-24).

As an act of love, God has always warned people to alert them to the right choices they needed to make. During the days of Israel's kings, he warned people through his prophets. They said things like, "Your hands are covered with blood. Wash yourselves, make yourselves clean; remove the evil of your deeds from my sight. Cease to do evil, learn to do good. But if you refuse and rebel, you will be devoured by the sword" (Isaiah 1:15-20). "Woe to those who call evil good, and good evil. . . . Who justify the wicked for a bribe, and take away the rights of the ones who are in the right" (Isaiah 5:20-25). "I have sent to you all my servants the prophets, sending them again and again, saying 'Turn now every man from his evil way and amend your deeds, and do not go after other gods to worship them.' . . . but you have not inclined your ear or listened to me" (Jeremiah 35:15). God gave his people opportunity after opportunity to repent. In the end, God's people failed him, and as God had warned, they were taken into captivity by their enemies, the walls of their beloved city, Jerusalem, were broken down, and their temple was destroyed. Thus it happened that God punished his own people, allowing them to be taken captive by enemy nations and exiled into foreign lands (2 Kings 17:5-18; Jeremiah 25:1-11).

God wants to save all people and nations, not punish and destroy. In the days of kings and prophets, God's wars occurred many times. He sent warning messages by his prophets not only to Israel and Judah but to other nations as well. For example, Jeremiah was a prophet to many nations (Jeremiah 1:4-5; 25:15-26). Another prophet, Jonah, went to warn Nineveh, the capitol city of Assyria, about God's coming judgment. They were enemies of Israel, and Jonah was angry when they repented and God did not destroy them. God asked Jonah, "Do you have good reason to be angry? Should I not have compassion on Nineveh, the great city in which there are more than 120,000 persons . . . as well as many animals?" (Jonah 4:4, 11). God spoke these words through the prophet Isaiah: "In the last days the mountain of the house of the Lord will be established as the chief of the mountains. All nations will stream to it. And many peoples will come and say, 'Let us go to the mountain of the Lord that he may teach us concerning his ways and that we may walk in his paths.' And he will judge between nations and they will hammer their swords into plowshares and their spears into pruning hooks. Nation will not lift up sword against nation, and never again will they learn war" (Isaiah 2:2-4).

God's love gives hope not only to Israel but to all people everywhere. God promises that he will fulfill all his promises to Israel. Although in captivity, he would bring them back to their homeland. This he did through the kings of Persia. Those kings included Cyrus, c.576–529 (Ezra 1:1-3; 3:10-11) and King Artaxerxes, c.464–425 (Nehemiah 2:1-8). Permission from those kings allowed the Jews to return to their homeland and be free to govern themselves, but they remained under the rule of Persia, then Greece, and then Rome, into the times of Christ. This period of Israel's kings and prophets ends, and we don't hear from God through his prophets for a period of about four hundred years. Then comes the days of the Messiah to fulfill his promise to Abraham that "in you all the families of the earth will be blessed" (Genesis 12:3).

THE TIMES OF CHRIST JESUS

When the long-prophesied Messiah came, his people did not recognize him (John 1:11). Instead, they rejected him and crucified him (Acts 2:22-23, 36; 13:27-28). He said, "O Jerusalem, Jerusalem, who kills the prophets and stones those who are sent to her! How often I wanted to gather your children together; the way a hen gathers her chicks under her wings, and you were unwilling. Behold, your house is being left to you desolate" (Matthew 23:37-38). Later, when approaching the city, and nearing the time of his death, he prophesied, "For the days will come upon you when your enemies . . . will level you to the ground and your children within you, and they will not leave in you one stone upon another, because you did not

81

recognize the time of your visitation" (Luke19:41-44). He once told his disciples that their temple would be torn down (Matthew 24:1-2). Thus it happened in AD 70 that the Roman army fulfilled these prophesies, and the Israelite people were scattered throughout many nations. They were no longer a nation until, amazingly, in 1948, they were restored to their promised land (see Luke 21:20-24). Israel has been constantly under threat of extinction from enemy nations, but even in modern times, God helped their nation to remain secure. For example, against all odds, during their 1967 war, soldiers allegedly witnessed miracles that enabled them to defeat their enemies. God still has a plan for Israel, and they are still looking forward to the coming of their Messiah.

Because his people rejected him, Jesus said to the Jewish religious leaders of his day, "The kingdom of God will be taken away from you and given to a people producing the fruit of it" (Matthew 21:43). One of Israel's purposes was to reach other nations with the message of God's love and salvation. However, they did not do a consistent job of this, a key reason being that they lacked a heart of love for God, always wandering away from him, worshiping and serving the gods of other nations. God longed for them to have a heart to love and serve him (Deuteronomy 5:29; Psalm 81:13), and he promised to give them such a heart by putting his Spirit within them (Ezekiel 36:21-27; Joel 2:28-32). This they perhaps could have had if they would have accepted Jesus as their Messiah, but it will be fulfilled for Israel at a later time (Romans 11:25-26; Luke 21:24).

The times of Jesus did not end with his death. He came back to life and is creating his church, a people made up of believers from all nations (Matthew 16:18; 1 Peter 2:9-10; Revelation 5:9). They share his message of salvation—doing his work on earth until he comes again (Acts 1:8-11).

GOD'S WARS ARE FOUGHT DIFFERENTLY TODAY

Like God's people in olden days, with God's help, the church is to resist the evil ways of the world and fight God's wars. However, in these days of Christ Jesus, God's wars are fought differently. Rather than physical fighting, people of the church are to overcome evil and establish God's goodness by receiving Christ through faith, practicing God's love as Jesus lived and taught (1 John 2:3-11) and sharing God's message of salvation with the peoples of the world (Matthew 28:18-20). Although Christ's followers must do battle with God's enemies, they are to fight God's wars in new ways. The battle plan is for his people to put on the full armor of God so that the church will be able to stand against evil forces. God's armor, including weapons, is spiritual in nature. It includes God's words of truth, faith in God and his truth, God's righteousness, the hope of salvation, proclaiming the gospel of peace, and prayer (Ephesians 6:10-18). God's people are to fight a spiritual war against evil on three fronts: the devil and his satanic forces, one's inner self, and the world's evil lures and threats. Following are brief thoughts about these three areas of combat.

First, we war with the devil and his satanic forces (Ephesians 6:11-12). Like he did to the Lord Jesus (Luke 4:1-13), the devil tempts us and tries to get us to yield to his deceptive evils. We are attacked by the devil's temptations, including wrong and bad thoughts, and his accusations (Revelation 12:10-11). He wants to destroy us and God's work. The way to have him flee is to resist these temptations and thoughts as soon as they enter our mind. Say to the evil one, *No, I'm not going there, I will not think those things. Leave me alone.* Then, immediately replace those thoughts with thoughts God wants you to have, perhaps a scripture verse, thoughts of good things God has done for you, thanks to him for particular blessings in your life, or a prayer for someone. The earlier you can recognize a satanic voice and have a plan to resist it, the easier it will be to overcome any negative results that come from hanging on to those thoughts. God's people have the authority from Jesus to resist the devil and other evil spirits, and they will flee (1 Peter 5:8-9; James 4:7).

Our second war is within ourselves (Galatians 5:16-17). When we become a follower of Jesus, he gives us his Holy Spirit (John 1:33; 4:10-14; 7:37-39; Acts 2:16-21, 38; Romans 8:9). Now we have two natures: the old self-centered character of our sinful nature and God's divine nature (2 Peter 1:3-4). Our battle is to overcome character defects and fight against bad habits—those things out of tune with God's love and goodness. For example, we must battle selfishness, bitterness, unforgiveness, jealousy, impatience, carousing, anger, greed, addictions, negativity, and so forth. Instead of these, we are to learn to live in the power of God's Spirit and grow into Christ-like character (Romans 8:29). His character includes love, peace, self-control, patience, goodness, kindness, faithfulness, and so forth (Ephesians 4:22-24; Galatians 5:19-25).

To let the power of God's Spirit empower us for daily living, we need to develop a habit of setting our minds on the things of the Spirit (Romans 8:5-14). For example, if you are going into a difficult situation and need God's help, you can say a prayer for God to fill you with his Spirit and help you think and do what he wants you to think and do, trusting him to be there helping you. Living in the Spirit becomes more natural to us as we hang out with God and Jesus by reading and learning the Bible. His words will become second nature in our thinking, and we will find ourselves changing into the ways God would have us think and act (Romans 12:1-2).

Another way to learn to walk in the Spirit is to be in close connection with other believers, through a church, a friend, or a small group. Others greatly affect our lives, whether negative or positive. Relationships are vitally important for our lives to become more Godlike (1 Corinthians 15:33; Hebrews 3:12-13; 10:24-25).

The third battle we face is a war against the influences of the world around us (1 John 2:15-17). The culture we live in and many of the people around us are constantly influencing us in a worldly direction. We are bombarded with various philosophies and religions telling us the best way to live. From social media, internet, TV, radio, and otherwise, we hear the voices of people telling us what we need to think or do concerning our health or lifestyle. We also encounter pressure from peers and others to join them in activities we feel ill at ease in doing. There are constant ads and presentations that appeal to us to buy and increase our material possessions (Colossians 3:2). God warns us to guard ourselves from idols—that is, anything that takes first place over God in our lives (1 John 5:21; Deuteronomy 5:7). We are in the world but not of it (John 17:14-16; 1 John 2:15-17; 1 Peter 2:11-12; James 4:4). The truth is, we don't have to own the world now because those who love and have faith in God shall one day inherit the world (Romans 4:13; 8:20-21; 2 Peter 3:13).

At present, Jesus teaches us that our war is a spiritual war, not a physical holy war against people who don't believe as we do and who we may want to force to conform to Christ's ways. Christ said he did not come to judge the world but to save the world (John 12:47). In these days of Christ Jesus, it is not our job to judge and destroy people for their sins. Rather, God wants the church to demonstrate to the world what his kingdom is like. It is a kingdom of love, peace, righteousness, and joy.

The church has made some mistakes during its history. For example, the church has mistakenly thought that her job was to bring God's physical kingdom on earth. To do that, the church did more than serve as a conscience to governments but coerced kings to be under their authority, dictating God's will for them. The church has also used force to make people into Christians, and they engaged in physical wars to take back holy lands they said belonged to them. But these are not God's ways in the days of Christ Jesus. The church makes disciples of Jesus through preaching the gospel and teaching those who believe to obey the Lord and to love all people and to do good. Sometimes, short of violence, love must stand against evil practices and help to protect people from injustices, and the Lord's voice needs to be heard. There will be a kingdom of God on earth, and the church is growing, being made up of people from every nationality, race, and economic status. But the kingdom will be fully created when Jesus comes again in person to complete God's salvation plan for the world. Christ will rule as King without end (Isaiah 9:6-7; Daniel 7:13-14; Luke 1:31-33).

Does living in this present age of truth and grace mean there will never again be a God war to bring God's justice and physically destroy the wicked? Not at all. After a lengthy time of peaceably inviting people to repent and believe in Jesus (Mark 1:14-15; 2 Peter 3:9), the Bible prophesies that the world will become increasingly hostile to God and his people. The church and Israel will face great persecution. God will again step in with justice, eliminating wickedness from the world and ushering in a righteous and peaceful world. Believers who have died at the hands of the wicked will be raised to life and will reign with Christ. Israel is not left out of God's plan, but when Jesus comes again at the end of this age to fight God's final war on behalf of his people, he will rescue them from their enemies and fulfill all promises to them (Zechariah 14:1-9; Revelation 19:11-16; Daniel 2:40-45; 7:13-27; 2 Thessalonians 1:3-10). Knowing the direction that the world is going these days, we say, "Amen, come Lord Jesus" (Revelation 22:20).

CHAPTER SUMMARY

We have learned that God does not destroy people without good and righteous reason. God fights to destroy those who are enemies for at least three reasons. First, he fights to promote social justice, judging and eliminating extreme wickedness in order to make the world a safer and better place. Why he intervenes to overthrow evil in some cases and not others is unknown to us. He works to achieve social justice through people who are his agents. His people in every church throughout the world have projects that God has put in their hearts to do to make people's lives better, and it is amazing to witness the good things God is doing through them all over the world. Others, besides God's people, also join in to help people who are suffering or hurting, but many people in this world are more destructive than good. They fail at being a part of God's work because of their self-centered pursuits or wickedness. Working for social justice never ends in an imperfect world. God calls us to keep overcoming evil by doing good (Romans 12:21).

Second, because he has instructed his people to carry out a task, he fights to protect them when his task is threatened and their lives are endangered. In times of trouble, it is natural to cry out to him for help. The promises and hope and help that God gives to them serves to sustain and comfort them. He promises that nothing will be able to stop his good and perfect plan or can separate them from what he has promised them (Romans 8:28-39). Again, he may not intervene in every case as we want, but many, when in trouble, testify that he has heard their cry and has saved them. All are encouraged to cry out to God for help in times of need and believe that God is faithful, no matter what happens (Hebrews 4:16).

Third, God has a plan to redeem his world, and he fights to guarantee its success. Satan, by finding ways to destroy the coming of the promised Messiah, has continuously tried to keep God's plans of salvation from happening. For example, King Herod, at the birth of Jesus, tried to kill him rather than have another person take his position of power. In spite of God's wars against wickedness, we have seen that God is not quick to destroy the wicked but is patient, giving warnings and opportunities for them to repent and be spared from his wrath (Ezekiel 18:32; John 3:16, 36; 2 Peter 3:9). God wants people to believe in him, be redeemed, and receive a new life, but he does not leave his enemies unpunished. Love is not love if, in the end, it allows evil to destroy what God loves. Many get away with evil in this world, and whether judgment day comes now or later, it is coming, and no one gets away with anything (Matthew 10:5-15; 12:36; Hebrews 9:27-28).

Believers are to trust God for their victory over evil. They are not to cower in the face of opposition but "be strong in the Lord and in the power of his might" (Ephesians 6:10). We have seen the Lord's power and might in the wars he fights. He performs miracles on behalf of his people, saving them from their enemies. We are not to fight our own battles in our own strength; rather, we are to rely on God's strength in our war against evil. This must be how we think. We know God is on our side, and when we join him in his war, we are confident he is there to help us. We do not give up and quit. We do not despair and withdraw in fear. His power and might, his promises to be with us, and knowing his future plans, strengthen us for battle. Sometimes it seems that bad things are happening and we are losing. We must determine to stand fast, knowing God will come through. Keep believing and trusting his help will come in his time and way. Psalm 73 gives hope when God seems against us and wickedness seems to be winning.

We, his people, have a mighty God who is for us in all the battles we face in life. "Greater is he who is in you than he who is in the world" (1 John 4:4). No one and nothing that comes against us can ultimately defeat us. God is our all-powerful warrior; he fights for us, and he will never let us be defeated, not even when death darkens our door (Psalm 23:4-6; Matthew 10:28; Esther 4:16; Daniel 3:13-18). "Who will separate us from the love of Christ? Will tribulation, or distress, or persecution, or famine, or nakedness, or peril, or sword? But in all these things, we overwhelmingly conquer through Him who loved us" (Romans 8:35-39). Faith, hope, and love are the mainstays in our walk with our warrior God, who equips us to be part of his victory to redeem and create a renewed world.

CHAPTER 5

LOVE IN THE CHURCH

A church was having problems with declining attendance and visitors not staying. Concerned individuals visited with people currently attending or some who had attended to try and discover what they thought about the church. Many commented that they felt like they were being judged and not accepted. Who wants to hang around a place that makes you feel unacceptable? I am acquainted with another church that had dwindled to a few people. The church had a reputation in the community of immorality in the church. Who wants to be in a church that does not practice what it is supposed to be teaching? Another church was dealing with an issue where people were taking sides, creating a church that lacked unity. Unfortunately, churches that resist and grieve the Spirit of God tend to repel people rather than attract them.

CONQUERING SIN IN THE CHURCH

What would you say are the most important things God wants his people to be concerned about and to practice? One way to answer this is to ask why God sent Jesus into the world. Jesus said he came to seek and save the lost (Luke 19:10). Specifically, he came to save us from our sins (Matthew 1:21; John 1:29). That being true, then sin ought to be a primary focus for the people of his church. If Jesus wants it gone from our lives, then we too must want it gone.

Long ago, God used his prophet to warn righteous people not to turn away from righteousness. He warned them that they should not sin (Ezekiel 3:21). The Apostle John said the same. He wrote in a letter to the church, "You know that He [Jesus] appeared in order to take away sins; and in Him there is no sin. No one who abides in Him sins; no one who sins has seen Him or knows Him . . . the one who practices sin is of the devil; for the devil has sinned from the beginning. . . . No one who is born of God practices sin" (1 John 3:5-6, 8-9). Sin was the cause of the problems described in this chapter's opening paragraph. One church was judgmental. Although it is not a sin to make right judgments about people, being judgmental toward them is a sin (John 7:24; Matthew 7:1-2). The other church allowed immorality. Immorality of any kind is wrong in a Christian's life, for we are to be holy as God is holy (1 Peter 1:14-16). The third church fought over certain issues. Disagreement is not necessarily a sin. Failing to preserve loving unity with people who differ with us is a sin (Ephesians 4:1-3).

Obviously no one is perfect. All people sin, including believers in Christ. Therefore, some clarification needs to be made concerning sin and righteousness. John's letter telling us not to sin does not mean we will always be able to keep sin from happening (1 John 2:1-2). It means we are not to habitually keep sinning but do all we can to correct our sinful attitudes, thoughts, and behaviors. There are two ways that we are righteous before God, and we need both. The first way is to be declared righteous by God. Read Romans 4 to see how God can declare us "not guilty." When God credits righteousness to us, we are forgiven all our sins. The Apostle Paul, in Philippians 3:9, tells us that being declared righteous means, "not having a righteousness of my own derived from Law [keeping God's laws], but that which is through faith in Christ, the righteousness which comes from God on the basis of faith." God credits us to be righteous in his sight when we have faith in what Jesus did on the cross. The second way to be righteous before God is to do God's will and practice his teachings. We voluntarily obey God out of humble gratitude for what God in Christ has done to save us. To know what a righteous life looks like, consider Job, a man God said was a righteous man. Job is a great example of what it means to be righteous in practice. Read Job 31.

The bottom line concerning sin is this: we need both ways of being righteous—God's declaring us "not guilty" and our practice of doing what is right. Being forgiven allows us to avoid putting ourselves down when we sin, thinking that we have failed and are no good. Instead, we can rise above our guilt or shame, moving on to become better. Whenever we sin, we admit our wrong to God, believe we are forgiven (1 John 1:9; 2:1), and then keep doing all we can to not repeat our sin (1 John 3:2-3). Romans 6:1-2 says, "Are we to continue in sin so that grace may increase? May it never be! How shall we who died to sin still live in it?" To learn the proper attitude and right thinking about sin, read Romans 5, 6, and 8:1-8. Yes, Jesus came to save us from our sin. Therefore, we need to take sin seriously and not let it destroy us and others. If we allow God to help us recognize our sins, and if we deal with our sins by seeking to eliminate them from our daily living, then we make room for love and peace to thrive in our relationships.

PUTTING GOD FIRST IN THE CHURCH: WHO'S THE BOSS?

Besides saving us from sin and its life-destroying consequences, there is another important thing Jesus came to do. He came to die so we could be reconciled to God through his death (Romans 5:10-11). Reconciliation means that our relationship with God has been restored, and we are at peace with God. We were estranged from God and subject to God's wrath (John 3:36), but now we know him, and we are in personal fellowship with the Father and with his Son, Jesus Christ, as well as with fellow believers (1 John 1:3). The result of Jesus saving us from sin and reconnecting us with God is that we are changed and given a heart to love God and one another as never before. God is supposed to be the number one person in our lives. Jesus said the two greatest commandments in life are to love God with our whole being and our neighbor as ourselves (Matthew 22:37-39).

If Jesus came to restore our relationship with God, then our relationship with God must become a primary focus. Now that Jesus has put us back in touch with God, the more we hang around with the God who is love the more his love will become part of us. How do we hang out with God? We do things together, just as we would with any friend or family member. We talk to him throughout the day, as if he were alongside of us, which he is. He is present with us to help us all day long. We get to know him better by reading about him in the Bible, thinking about him, even asking questions and searching for his answers. Who we hang around and spend time with has a lot to do with the kind of persons we become (Proverbs 27:17; 1 Corinthians 15:33). We know how wonderful and fulfilling it is to be loved by someone, and God has loved us more than anyone ever could (1 John 3:1). Did not God give us his love (Romans 5:5)? Did not our Lord command us to love one another as he has loved us (John 13:34)? If we love because he first loved us (1 John 4:19), why is it that we are so often at odds with people in the church? Where is the love for God and one another that he has given us?

If Jesus came to reestablish our relationship with God so that our relationship with God is now our primary focus, will we not want to love and please him? How do we show God we love him? We love God by "keeping his commandments; and his commandments are not burdensome" (1 John 5:3). To love and please the Lord in our daily living means correcting anything that displeases him—or should I say, that puts us at odds with his will and teachings. One day I lied to a person in the community, and I wrestled with God that night because he wanted me to go and tell the person what I did and ask his forgiveness. Because of my pride, I did not want to do it, but the next day I did. The man to whom I admitted my wrong asked me why I would come to him and do this. I said, "It's because I have a relationship with God, and He wanted me to make it right with you.

I don't want anything to interrupt and spoil my relationship with God. He trusts me to please him by doing what he says is right and good." Love in the church happens when we die to our prideful self and love and obey God above all else.

ALL KINDS OF PEOPLE IN THE CHURCH

Are believers doing a good job of practicing the love of God toward fellow believers? I wonder this because, although love is often practiced in churches, it is also not practiced, and that non-practice of God's love leads to hard feelings and divisions between church people. People who need to be loved feel ignored or shunned. Church splits happen when people cannot get along. What causes people in churches to be unloving and unaccepting of each other? There are many reasons. A lack of love can come from personality differences, a lack of social skills, disagreements over doctrinal issues, being critical of the moral or ethical lifestyles of others, not knowing what it means to grow in Christ, or being angered and unforgiving toward people who offend us in any number of ways. It is difficult to love people in the church when we are all different from each other, and not only different, but each of us has learned wrong behaviors from the hurtful events throughout our lives.

What was God thinking to put such a variety of people together and expect them to get along? God was thinking that we are all broken people who need healing. Jesus overheard others criticizing him for spending time with sinners. His reply was that the healthy do not need a physician, but the sick do (Mark 2:15-17). We all come from backgrounds having some degree of damaged and messed-up lives, leaving us with guilt, shame, warped personalities, or ungodly habits. We have been hurt and scarred by the evils of this world. Healing comes from being loved and accepted. Through that healing, we become loving, kind, patient, peaceful, happy, self-controlled, and good to the point where each of us has something of great value to give to each other and to the world around us. Through our faith and the grace of God, he is our healer, and we can become instruments he works through in the process of helping to heal one another.

WHAT IT MEANS TO BE THE BODY OF CHRIST

There is a chapter in God's Word, 1 Corinthians 12, that helps us develop a right understanding about the church and what God wants our attitude and actions toward one another to be. In that chapter the church is compared to a human body. The human body is one body with many parts. Each part contributes something to the life, health, and overall well-being of the whole body. The church is the same. It is Christ's body with many parts, each part having a function that contributes to the body's life, health, and well-being. Our human body has a head and brain that determines how the body thinks and acts. Likewise, Christ's body has a head, who is Christ Jesus, and he tells the parts of the body how he wants us to think and act. The parts of our human body differ from each other, just as the church people differ from one another, but each part has something that the body needs for helping the entire body function as God created it to function. We cannot say that any part of the body is not needed. We honor all parts by taking care of them. Each person in Christ's body has something to do in caring for the well-being of the church and the world around them.

Division is not to be part of the body (1 Corinthians 1:10). Can you imagine a part of your body separating itself from the other parts? Suppose your heart no longer wanted to be part of your body. Without the heart, the body dies. Suppose you decide you do not need one of your legs. With one leg missing, your body is crippled in what it can do. Suppose your body is injured and is bleeding, and your hand refuses to obey what the brain is telling it to do by applying ointment and a bandage to prevent infection and control the bleeding. The hand doesn't even think about not helping, for the head sends a message, and the hand automatically goes into action because it feels the discomfort and need in another part of the body. The parts of our body care for the other parts, so it is in the church (1 Corinthians 12:25).

Furthermore, our human body does not just care for itself; it regularly reaches out to give to others what is good and needed. Christ's body operates the same way, ministering not only to each other but also to people outside the church.

How do we maintain the unity and health of Christ's body? God gives us his Spirit to motivate, equip, and empower us to do his will. When we trust Jesus to save us, he baptizes us with his Spirit (Mark 1:7-8; 1 Corinthians 12:13). Each of us is adopted into God's family and is thereby a part of his body. Each of us is a gift to the church, for God, by his Spirit, has gifted us with talents and ministries to be discovered and used to make a difference for good, both in the church and in the world (1 Corinthians 12:18). Every person in the body of Jesus is also to pursue love as defined in 1 Corinthians 13. Everything we do is to be done in love. God provides the people who are needed to help his body grow and become healthy. With the help God supplies, we can work through our painful backgrounds, grow into healthy persons, and become one body, united in love (John 13:35; 17:20-23). We must not hinder that love by allowing self-centeredness and sin to control our lives. We must learn to walk in the Spirit (Galatians 5:16).

DIFFERING BELIEFS, OPINIONS, AND LIFESTYLES

Besides not understanding how the church body is to function and how to walk in the Spirit, another reason people do not get along in churches is their differing beliefs. When others do not believe what we believe, we can become argumentative, disturbed, or critical, or even look for another church body where people will agree and believe as we do. Serious differences in belief are of two kinds. There are differing beliefs in ethics and in doctrines. Ethically, we believe in something God says is the right or wrong way for us to live. What is an acceptable activity for some may not be OK for others, so we may judge another because they don't live the way we think they should.

There are also significant disagreements in churches over what the Bible says about various doctrines. That is a huge reason why there are Baptists, Methodists, Reformists, Episcopalians, Lutherans, Seventh-Day Adventists, non-denominationalists, Roman Catholics, and so forth. For example, one church may say that once a person is saved, they cannot lose their salvation, while another may say we can lose our salvation. Most churches worship on Sunday, but some say we must worship on Saturday. Churches believe different things about baptism, or they argue over end-times teachings concerning the Second Coming of Jesus. People in a church will split off and start another church over such differences. They think, *We have the truth and they don't, and we can't believe and teach the real truth in that group of people.* I am not suggesting some church splits are not warranted. Some are, but with helpful biblical teachings, as in Romans 14, on how God would have us deal with those who differ from us, divisive differences or splits may not have to happen. I am also not suggesting that a person must stay in one place and not go to another, but if there is valid reason for leaving, it is best if the separation can be done in love by all parties.

How does Romans 14 help us to preserve love and unity when in the church there are differing ethical or doctrinal beliefs? In this passage, two examples of differing beliefs are presented. The first example is over what a person should eat or not eat. In the early days of the church, the meat of an animal offered as a sacrifice to idols was, by some, considered unholy and should not be eaten. To avoid eating such meat, they ate only vegetables. Others of the faith said there are no such things as idols, for there is only one true and living God, therefore all things are lawful to eat (Romans 14:2). The second example (Romans 14:5) involves days some think should be observed as special days for honoring God, while others think every day should be honoring to God. Differing ethical or doctrinal issues can cause friction.

Many churches and individuals in our day have what I like to call, "pet doctrines." They strongly believe and teach things in the Bible are true, even though they are controversial as is evidenced by others who hold different views based on the same Bible. Examples include the following: Some churches teach that a special "baptism of the Holy Spirit," as a second work of God's grace, is necessary in order to have power to live the Christian life, while others do not. Some churches emphasize the sovereignty of God in determining who is saved, while others emphasize the role of free will in salvation. Concerning water baptism, some churches believe in baptizing infants, while others insist that adult baptism is the only way. Some persons would say attending a movie theater is wrong, while others say it is not. We may not realize it, but if we have been raised in a church or attended that church's school system and have learned that church's beliefs and ways, we are likely to find it difficult to be in loving unity with church people who differ from us. Instead of allowing ethical and doctrinal differences to hinder love for one another, is it possible to acquire God's mind through his Word, learn ways of overcoming differences, and bring loving unity to the church?

Jesus was concerned about unity in his body, and he prayed that God would make us one in him (John 17:20-21). Our oneness in a sinful world is not based on all agreeing about all the same things and having all the same ideas. It's about accepting and loving one another in spite of our differences, helping each other grow in our faith, and living our daily lives according to God's will. There are things in all churches that would divide us, but unity in the Spirit should be our goal, and we should learn to achieve success at being unified in Christ (Ephesians 4:1-3).

God gave Romans 14 to help us develop the kind of thinking that allows us to love and be with people who have differing beliefs. This does not mean we must be tolerant and unconcerned about heretical Bible beliefs or sinful lifestyles (Revelation 2:12-17). Certainly, some things are unacceptable and need to be addressed, but beyond that, we must recognize the difference between more-essential and less-essential truths in God's Word and wisely learn when and why it is OK to allow differences. Our goal is to build one another up in the faith, not tear each other down and cause divisions over differences. In light of the problems caused by differing ethics and doctrines, let us see what God teaches us in Romans 14 about how we can accept one another and be one in Christ.

In Romans 14:1, there is need to recognize that there are persons weak in faith and others who are strong in faith. This has nothing to do with the sincerity of each person in loving God and wanting to follow and obey Jesus as their Lord. Both weak and strong are committed to Christ and want to do his will. The difference is that some need more information about their faith, while others have a more complete or accurate understanding of the faith (Acts 18:24-26). In order for any person to be open to learning more, it helps if they are accepted and are given time and grace to learn and grow. We are all at different places in our faith; we all need to learn more, both in our beliefs and in our practice of those beliefs. God knows when we are ready to receive certain things he wants to teach us or when we are not yet ready. The first thing Paul says is that if we think we are the strong one, we need to make sure the one we think is weak in faith feels loved and accepted.

The second thing Paul teaches is that the one who has more information and feels the need to correct the other is not to regard that person with contempt. Visa-versa, the one who may need more information in their faith is not to judge the one who they feel makes them out to be less of a Christian. Each person is to be fully convinced in his or her own mind about what they believe is God's word and will for them. Each is to stop passing judgment on the other's opinions, beliefs, or way of life. Why? Because, Paul says, "God has accepted them" (Romans 14:3). Neither one is living for him or herself, but each is claiming to be living for the Lord. Who are we to judge the servant of another? To his own master, each one stands or falls. God is our judge. Each of us is responsible to him for what we believe and how we live. We are the Lord's; therefore, why do we judge our fellow believer? Or, why do we regard our fellow believer with contempt? "We will all stand before the judgment seat of God" (Romans 14:10), and each of us will give an account of him or herself to God (Romans 14:12).

Third, Paul says that instead of judging one another, we ought to determine not to put an obstacle or a stumbling block in a fellow believer's way (Romans 14:13). An obstacle or stumbling block might be to say and imply to the other that he or she is not believing or living the right way. If this would cause them to feel uncertain about their beliefs or actions to the point that they have guilt or shame or doubts or feel unaccepted and unloved, are we not causing them to stumble in their faith? Are we not putting a block between us and them by causing a strained relationship? Are we not damaging our oneness in Christ?

A friend shared with me that he had been in a small group for a few years with a fellow believer who continuously stressed the need for the others in the group to believe and practice his certain biblical way of living. My friend always felt unaccepted and that he was not a good Christian. This hindered his confidence in his faith and put a strain on his relationships in the body of Christ. One day, he could take it no longer and shared in the group how this made him feel wrong in his faith and unaccepted. It was discussed by members in the group, and the person with such a strong belief was gracious enough to be honest and admit that it was not good to make a fellow believer feel this way. The group was better for the open and honest discussion, and there was a deeper love for one another and openness to learn from one another.

If we want love in the church to increase more and more (1 Thessalonians 3:12), we need to understand how the expression of our beliefs or lifestyles affects others. We need to be careful that we are not hurting others by judging and destroying them, trying to change them to please ourselves, and thinking we are doing God's work by bringing them in line with our beliefs and practices. This is not walking in love (Romans 14:15).

The kingdom of God is righteousness and peace and joy in the Holy Spirit. We are to pursue the things that make for peace and the building up of one another. Each of us must always be checking to make sure that what we believe and practice is according to our faith in God's Word. Each must have his or her own conviction before God and must not be condemning themselves in what they believe. There are times for appropriately confronting persons about something that is not right, but if a person is believing and doing what God wants them to believe and do, according to what they truly believe God's Word says or teaches, we need to give them permission to believe differently than we do, so long as it is not sinful.

A good exercise to help us apply the proper loving attitude toward one who disagrees with us is to take your own belief and their belief and plug it into Romans 14:3, substituting your issue in the place of the issue of *eating meat* that Paul presents in the verse. Here is an example: "The one who believes in [*adult baptism*] is not to regard with contempt the one who believes in [*infant baptism*], and the one who believes in [*infant baptism*] is not to judge the one who believes in [*adult baptism*]." Now it's your turn to fill in the blanks with whatever difference you are having with another. Insert your belief and their belief in the following designated spaces:

The one who believes in (put in your belief) is not to regard with contempt the one who believes in (put in their belief), and the one who does not believe in (put in their belief) is not to judge the one who believes in (put in your belief).

Again, accepting the other person with their beliefs does not mean you are accepting their beliefs. It means you are practicing the Lord's principles of love and unity. Success at unity requires humility. We all need to be open to other ideas and willing to change our thinking if another's ideas seem right according to God's Word. If we don't agree, it is all right to have our faith in God's Word as we see it, for we are all responsible to God, and to God we stand or fall.

It is also good to share and discuss with others what we believe and why. All of us at times acquire new understanding, and we change our beliefs when we continue to study God's Word and listen to others' views. Remember, each of us as sincere followers of Jesus loves and serves the Lord, and each of us will answer to him for our faithfulness, no matter if it agrees with others or is different from others.

DIFFERING PERSONALITIES AND SOCIAL BACKGROUNDS

Another problem that hinders church people from loving one another is a clash of personalities or social status. James addresses this issue in his biblical letter, James 2:1-9, where he says it is sin to make distinctions in how we treat one person over another. How do we love people we do not want to be around because of their personalities or lifestyles? It is natural for people to be attracted to others with like interests, social status, or agreeable personalities. However, what if they are obnoxious, offensive, unfriendly, or whatever? We do not have to be everyone's close friend. But, as believers in Christ, we are called to love and build up one another. Granted, it's not easy to be around some people. Remember, due to a sinful world and imperfect or evil-filled upbringings, we all have personalities that are to some degree, shall I say, warped or distorted. To help us accept differing or offensive personalities, rather than judging, it is helpful to learn enough about them to see the good in them. Focusing on their good qualities and their potential gives us a start to accepting and wanting to befriend and help them. As Jesus obeyed God by living to please others for their good and up-building, so we are to be like our Lord in not living to please ourselves but in accepting others, just as Christ has accepted us (Romans 15:7).

EASY TO OFFEND, DIFFICULT TO MEND

Finally, I want to address the fact that offending one another cannot be avoided. How do we know if we are offended? We know we have been offended or bothered by something or someone if, for example, we are critical, complaining, angry, feeling hurt, gossiping, argumentative, or avoiding someone. There is never a perfect church because it is made up of imperfect people. Because of so many differences in people and in the ways we do things, it is easy to be hurt by others or critical of things we see that bother us. A critical, complaining, angry, offended spirit serves to tear things down, not build them up. A critical spirit can be good and helpful if controlled by love and a desire to make things better, but that is often not what happens. To keep love and unity as a primary concern, one's critical spirit needs to be corrected (Colossians 3:13). When we all desire and try to develop loving relationships with people in the church, at a right time, we talk with each other about things that bother us. When we are aware of offending someone, or when we are offended, we are to engage in a forgiveness process. Lack of forgiveness allows problems in the church to fester and grow, thus hindering the healing work Christ wants to do in our own lives and in the lives of those around us. We can't stop wrong and offensive things from happening, but we can seek to correct them. Forgiveness is a huge mending tool. That is why forgiveness has its own chapter in this book.

Christ Jesus died not just for each of us as individuals but to create a community of people who share life together with God in his eternal kingdom. His kingdom is both here and now, and it is yet to come when Jesus returns and takes his place as King (Zechariah 9:9-10; 14:9). All who are truly of his church are transferred into his kingdom here and now (Colossians 1:13-14), and yet, we pray for and wait for his kingdom to come on earth as it is in heaven (Matthew 6:9-10). When Jesus was on earth, he demonstrated by his teaching, miracles, and life, something of what his kingdom is like. He wants his kingdom to be on earth as it is in heaven and his will to be done on earth as it is in heaven. He made his church to be a kingdom of priests who will show to the world what God and his kingdom is like (1 Peter 2:9-12). He made us into a people who will care about this world as God does. As a community of believers in this present world, we are to demonstrate something of what his kingdom is like so that others will also want and seek his kind of life for themselves.

GOD'S KINGDOM

What will God's heavenly kingdom be like? It will be a community with no sin. If we will have no sin in heaven, then let's stop sinning against one another now, in this present age of his kingdom. The kingdom of heaven will be unified around the leadership of Jesus our King, and we gladly and willingly will obey the laws of his kingdom. If we will gladly live by his teachings and ways there, let's together obey what he tells us to do now, in this present life. His kingdom consists of individuals from every tribe, tongue, people, and nation, mixed together as one (Revelation 5:9-10). If that is the mix of people in Christ's kingdom, there should be no racial, social, or economic discrimination among us now. God will have a community of people from all walks of life who will enjoy being with each other, appreciating and benefitting from one another's unique personalities and talents.

If that is the way it will be then, let's appreciate and enjoy the benefits we can receive from one another now, in this present life together. In his community, there will be no feelings of isolation and loneliness. If that is true, let's make sure no one feels alone and left out in the life we currently share together. In God's heavenly community, love will rule, and we will share who we are and what we have with one another, so let's share who we are and what we have for the good of one another now (Acts 4:32-35). God is Father, Son, and Holy Spirit, a complete social community of love within himself.

He created a people to be a community like himself, a community in harmonious fellowship with him and with each other, a community of faith, hope, and love (1 Corinthians 13:13). We are to care for the world as God cares for the world, by cooperating in his work of redeeming it.

PARTING THOUGHTS AND CHALLENGE

I do not blame people for whatever feelings they may have against the church. I sympathize with people who have been hurt by the church, perhaps falsely judged, rejected, or wronged in some other way. Many can point out the negative or erring side of churches. I too have experienced hurt in the church, and I have hurt others through my imperfections. But I have also seen all the good it can do. The church has been a big part of my life. I love the church because of something I once heard a respected teacher say. He said, "The church has its many faults and is far from perfect, but never forget that Jesus loved the church and died for her." However, just because I love the church does not mean I am satisfied with the way it is. There is always room for it to grow to the next level of what God wants it to be. I feel privileged that God has allowed me to have a part in her becoming a more perfect bride for Christ on the day he comes to receive her unto himself.

I challenge you to play your part. The church is not just somebody else; it is your own body. Take care of it. Our job description is clearly laid out in God's Word. If you need a renewed energy and love for the church, try reading and practicing Colossians 3:1-17. People entangled in hurtful and lost worldly ways need those in the church to bring the life of Jesus to them. Especially in our increasingly ungodly and lawless days, Jesus, through his church, offers people hope, love, and peace that can be found nowhere else.

CHAPTER 6

LOVE AND FORGIVENESS

Forgiveness is such a broad subject, one hardly knows where to begin. *When do I forgive, should I forgive, how do I forgive, why forgive, how do I get forgiven, how do I forgive myself,* and many other issues arise concerning forgiveness. People must deal with a wide variety of forgiveness situations that range from simple to complex. I will not be able to cover the entire subject of forgiveness in a chapter. There are many books and articles written about forgiveness that have value, and we can learn something helpful from each one. In this chapter I offer some beginning thoughts, some things God tells us in his Word, and some forgiveness stories from my own life, all of which you may find helpful as you work on your own forgiveness issues. As ever, the Bible is the primary source book on the subject; however, as I said, other books can be helpful, and later in the chapter I will mention one particular book that I found of much value.

WHAT IS FORGIVENESS?

Forgiveness, according to the Bible, is a release or dismissal of something. For example, in Matthew 18:27, forgiveness means to release someone from a debt of money owed so that it is no longer owed, thus freeing a person from its burden. In Acts 8:22, the evil intentions of one's heart need forgiven. Forgiveness is most often used for the release or dismissal of sins you are guilty of doing, or releasing someone else from wrongs done to you. To be released or dismissed from debts or sins is to have them completely cancelled. A primary purpose for Jesus coming to earth was to save people from their sins (Matthew 1:21; John 1:29; 1 John 3:5).

There are a few common phrases used in our culture that make forgiveness sound easy, statements like "forgive and forget," "let it go and move on," or if someone apologizes to you, all you need say is, "that's OK," and it's over. There are things forgiveness is and things forgiveness is not. Contrary to some peoples' thinking, forgiveness is not easy. It requires humility, grace, and working through hard feelings. It is not always in our human nature to forgive, especially when people keep wronging and hurting us. Actually, it is normal and right to be resistant toward wrongdoing and wrongdoers, for in truth, that is not God's will for people.

There is something about sin that is repulsive to God and us. Forgiveness does not mean we will automatically trust others or that we will always be reconciled and friends with people or that we will feel loving toward everyone or that we pretend everything is OK. Forgiveness is an act of our will that asks others to pardon our offenses against them, that pardons another for their offenses against us, or that pardons ourselves. It is an act that frees those involved from hurt, anger, and resentment, enabling people to love others instead of hurt them. Forgiveness can heal us mentally, emotionally, spiritually, physically, and relationally.

THREE REASONS FORGIVENESS IS NEEDED

There are three reasons why forgiveness is needed. First, forgiveness is needed *to be rid of guilt*. We all acquire guilt when we wrong God, ourselves, or others. Guilt is a terrible feeling that can make it hard to live with oneself. The psalm writer, David, said that guilt caused his vitality for living to be lost (Psalm 32:3-4). When David committed adultery and then had the woman's husband killed to cover it up, he first tried to dismiss it from his mind, but he could not, and the evil he did remained ever present in his conscience. He felt condemned and at odds with himself and God. David longed to have his guilt removed so he could feel clean and at peace (Psalm 51:1-17). We learn from David that forgiveness for guilt requires repentance; confession from an honest, sincere, and humbled heart; and faith to believe God forgives.

Second, forgiveness is needed *to restore damaged relationships.* Our offenses create bad feelings with others. God made us for love not for broken relationships. God wants us, as much as possible, to be at peace with all people. Sadly, people often do not care about broken relationships unless it involves someone they need or deeply care about. At a marriage seminar my wife and I attended, the speaker likened forgiveness to the reset button on the ball return at a bowling alley. When the pins are knocked down and need to be set up again, you push the reset button, and the pins are put back in place. Forgiveness is the reset button in our relationships—it sets things right again.

Third, Forgiveness is needed *to enter God's eternal kingdom* (Colossians 1:13-14). Because evil and wrongdoing does not exist in God's kingdom, there is only one way for sinners, meaning all of us, to be admitted. We must be forgiven, be declared righteous by God, be equipped with a new heart that desires to live a changed life, and be given an immortal body that no longer sins. This process begins with forgiveness and is completed when Jesus returns in glorious fashion to raise his people and receive them into his kingdom.

WHAT TO KNOW ABOUT THE GOD WHO FORGIVES

In the Bible, in both Old and New Testaments, God is a loving and forgiving God. His compassion and lovingkindness pardons our iniquities and casts our sins into the depths of the sea (Micah

7:18-19). God warned Israel that he will punish them, destroy their nation, and send them into captivity if they no longer listen to him, serve other gods, and live a sinful life. God reminds them that he is the one and only God, the one who created them as a nation to serve him and be a witness of his salvation to the world. When God sees the Israelites engaged in sinful lifestyles, he pleads with them to return to him, and he will forgive. Through the prophet Isaiah, he says, "You have burdened me with your sins, you have wearied me with your iniquities. I, even I, am the one who wipes out your transgressions for my own sake, and I will not remember your sins" (Isaiah 43:24-25). Although this offer of forgiveness was written to Israel, these words apply to all who repent and have faith in God, or in Jesus, for the forgiveness of their sins. These Old Testament truths apply to us as much as they applied to persons back then. This is because those who believe in God and Jesus have the same founding father as Israel and the same God. From the God of the Bible, no matter who we are or what we've done, his forgiveness is available to all who repent and come to him.

Jesus and the Bible have much to teach us about forgiveness. For Jesus, forgiveness is an essential lifestyle to develop. He taught his followers to pray for God to forgive them as they have forgiven others (Matthew 6:12). He explained, "For if you forgive others for their transgressions, your heavenly Father will also forgive you. But if you do not forgive others, then your Father will not forgive your transgressions" (Matthew 6:14-15). This is a difficult teaching to understand and accept, for we do not think of God as one who would take back his forgiveness. In a parable Jesus told in Matthew 18:23-35, he reaffirmed a rule of God's kingdom, that God will not forgive us if we do not forgive as we have been forgiven. In the parable, a wicked slave who was forgiven by his master would not forgive a fellow slave. The master was displeased with that wicked slave and handed him over to be tortured until he paid back what he owed.

Some have asked, *If we hold a grudge and do not forgive someone, does that mean we lose our forgiveness and salvation from God and cannot go to heaven?* Two thoughts: (1) The unforgiving servant may not have been a genuine believer, so he never had a place in heaven. (2) Notice that the punishment for the unforgiving slave was not to lose his place as a servant but to suffer torture until he settled his issue with him. We are to be kind to one another, tenderhearted, forgiving each other, just as God in Christ has forgiven us (Ephesians 4:32; Colossians 3:13). If we have received merciful forgiveness from God and have become relieved and grateful to God, it follows that we would naturally want to forgive others. We may not lose our salvation and be cast out of God's kingdom, but God is not pleased with us, and our fellowship with him remains disrupted until we forgive as we have been forgiven. Interestingly, when we know we should be forgiving but aren't, we can be mentally and emotionally tortured until we do. Peter asked Jesus, "Lord, how often shall my brother sin against me and I forgive him?" Jesus answered, "Up to seventy times seven" (Matthew 18:21-22). God wants us to take forgiveness seriously and learn to do it.

LESSONS FROM MY FORGIVENESS EXPERIENCES

An experience I had years ago taught me a lot about forgiveness. A friend and I spent lots of time fixing up a cabin, and it was vandalized. The cabin was in a wooded area next to a river. I went out one day and discovered that the locked door had been forced open. I went in and saw broken dishes from the cupboards that were strewn about, holes had been punched in the sheet rock walls, beer cans and garbage were tossed everywhere. Apparently, there had been a drinking party, and the place was trashed. I became so angry that I wanted to find out who did this and make them pay. The hatred I felt consumed me. I couldn't sleep at night. I thought of ways to get even, like rigging a gun at the door, hoping they would come again and be shot. I had no peace of mind. Then, one night while lying in bed, a gentle voice inside of me said, *I thought you were a Christian. How can you want to kill somebody?* This thought reminded me that, as a follower of Jesus, I needed to forgive them. Following are things I learned about forgiveness.

(1) *Forgiveness is hard.* I did not want to forgive because a wrong had been done. If I forgave, then they would not get the justice they deserved. I would not let them off the hook. As I thought about what they did, which was nearly every night, my feelings of vengeance and

the need to see them punished would not go away. Suddenly, one night, a Bible verse came to mind: "Vengeance is mine; I will repay says the Lord" (Romans 12:18-19). I said, *OK, Lord, I give them to you. If you want to punish them, you do it.* Turning wrongdoers over to God, believing he would punish as needed, was a step toward becoming able to forgive.

(2) *I have to think differently.* It is still hard to forgive. What helped me was to think differently about the people who did this. I did not know anything about them, but I began to wonder if they came from dysfunctional homes. Were they beaten or abused? Had they become slaves to alcohol? Did they ever have an opportunity to know the love of God? When I thought about their lives in a new light, I began to feel a little sorry for them. Having empathy and understanding softened me to the point where I became willing to forgive, so I decided to do it. I said, *God, I forgive whoever it was for destroying my property.* When I did this, I felt at peace for the first time in a long time. I learned that having hatred and resentment and bitterness was hurting and damaging me more than it was them (Hebrews 12:14-15). I needed to forgive not only for their sakes but for my own healing.

(3) *The wrongs don't just go away.* The next night, the thoughts of what they did came back into my mind, and I was angry all over again. I said to myself, *Wait a minute, I thought I forgave them. How come these thoughts of anger and revenge are still bothering me?* Immediately, I reminded myself that I did forgive them, and I sincerely meant it. I learned that forgiving does not mean the thoughts of what happened would be gone. It means that when they enter your mind, you do not allow them. It's like the devil wants to keep you angry to destroy your well-being. So I said, *I did forgive them, and I am not allowing these thoughts back into my mind.* I dismissed them and thought about something else. I was not bothered by them again. God says that when he forgives, he casts our sins as far away as east from west. He does not bring the past up again. Neither should I.

(4) I learned that *it costs to forgive.* Jesus paid a price to forgive those who crucified him. He paid by giving up his life for them so that they could be forgiven. If wrongdoers are forgiven when they know they don't deserve it, that experience can change their lives. In

110

the movie *Les Misérables*, a man recently released from prison found someone who gave him a place to stay for the night. When the man left the next morning, he stole some goods from the one who helped him. The next day, the police caught the thief and took him back to the man from whom he stole. Surprisingly, the man who was the victim of wrongdoing told the police that he gave those things to the thief. That act of forgiving mercy changed the thief into a new and honest man, dedicated to helping the needy. Of course, the one who did the forgiving had to assume the cost of losing his goods. In a small way, that is what I also had to do—take on the cost for someone else's wrongs. It seems unfair, and it is, but it is the reality of forgiving. Jesus was innocent but suffered the death others deserved. In my case also, the guilty did not have to pay for what they did. I had to assume the cost of fixing up my property and being OK with it. That is something love is willing to do.

(5) *The feelings will change.* In my situation, this is how I dealt with forgiveness when not knowing who was guilty. For all I know, they got away with their crime. Normally, forgiving does not mean excusing people, condoning their behavior, or letting them get away with wrongs. We can forgive and at the same time confront them and try to stop or help change what the wrongdoer is doing. After I forgave, I had further thoughts about those who wrecked my property. I thought, *If I met who wronged me, I feel like I would want to get to know them and try to help them.* I learned that the proof of having genuinely forgiven someone was that we would feel differently and want to love them instead of hurt them. This does not mean we would be friends. It takes two to reconcile with each other. If the other does not want to accept your forgiveness or help, so be it. At least you did your part before God, which freed you from being angry and hurtful, and it freed you to love others, even those who may not deserve it.

As long as I am relating things I've learned about forgiveness, I might as well share a different experience that taught me other things. This experience has to do with my hurting someone else and my need to be forgiven. I accompanied a group of kids to a kids' Olympic meet to compete in games with teams from other towns. It came down to the last game, and our team could win first place. It was a race of many laps around a game circle, and the first person to grab a pin in the middle of the circle was the winner. My daughter was in the race, and I told her I would count the laps for her so she would know when to go for the prize. She ran the laps, and when she thought she had run them all, she looked at me for the signal to run into the center. In my excitement of watching her, I lost track of the count and told her to run one more lap. She would have won, but everyone finished ahead of her, and the entire team lost the meet. I felt terrible. I felt totally responsible for her and her team losing. But causing their loss through a mistake I made was not what I felt most guilty about. I felt guilty that I had betrayed my daughter's trust. She trusted me, and I failed her. As I sat in the bus on the way home, a trip of 380 miles, that painful experience was all I could think about. Following are things from this experience that I learned about forgiveness.

(1) *Forgiveness means sorting out what happened and seeing how it affects every person involved.* I had to sort out what happened, why it happened and possible underlying causes, and how people felt or might have felt. To be rid of my guilt, I knew I had to ask my daughter, and the team, to forgive me for failing them. I decided to do this, for I had hurt them. They must have felt very disappointed in losing. But I wrestled with a deeper problem. *How do I forgive myself? How do I get over my hurting people I love and care about?* In thinking about this, I realized that as a sinful human, I am not perfect—I wrong others, and I make mistakes. I did not intend to betray my daughter's trust. It just happened because I got caught up in the race instead of doing my job. That could happen to anyone. Still, that did not excuse my failure. Actually, I was experiencing what is called *shame*. *Shame*, I am told, differs from *guilt*. Guilt is doing something wrong, and one must take responsibility for it. Shame is feeling bad and putting yourself down by telling yourself you are a bad, no-good person. I wondered, *Did I need forgiveness for being an imperfect human, something I couldn't help?*

(2) After sorting things out, I decided to ask God to forgive me for failing to be responsible and hurting others. So I asked his forgiveness. I know he forgave me, but I still did not feel good about it. I learned that *you cannot only ask God's forgiveness, but to*

have peace, you must also seek forgiveness from the ones you offended, sinned against, or hurt. It took being humble, denying my pride, and courage to stand and ask my daughter and the group to forgive me for what I did, but when I did, a wonderful thing happened. They all readily said it was OK. They forgave me. I felt our relationship was kept intact, and we could go on just as if the wrong had never occurred. Forgiveness gives us these blessings: broken relationship can be restored, others can be healed of bad feelings toward us, and we can feel relief and peace.

(3) I turned back to God to deal with my deeper issue of being an imperfect person. I realized that *Jesus did not only die on a cross so my sins could be forgiven, but his death also covered my being an imperfect person.* Jesus loves and accepts me as I am, with all my faults. I learned that I needed to accept myself because he did. I learned that I needed to be OK with being imperfect. That's what love does, even love for yourself. I do not have to put myself down or let others shame me for my faults. I can work on them to get better, and when I know I am loved as a less than perfect person, I can accept others' criticisms of me. God loves me. Whenever I fail to be perfect, I need to say to myself, *That's OK—accept the fact you are not perfect because Jesus accepts you. Just move on, trying to become better, and thank Jesus for loving you and dying for all that is wrong with you.* I realize some people have more serious things to work through, and forgiveness issues may take longer to resolve, but hopefully they end up at the same place. Just think, someday, as believers in Christ's promises, we will have new bodies in his glorious kingdom and will no longer have to deal with sin and imperfections.

THE POWER OF BEING LOVED AND ACCEPTED

A biblical story that Jesus told about a man and two sons teaches us some other important things about forgiveness (Luke 15:11-32). Both sons had a father who loved them, but they needed to learn the meaning of love, and it had to do with forgiveness. The first son decided that he would take money his father gave him and leave home. Evidently, he did not like life on the family farm and wanted to go out and live his life as he wanted. We call that *freedom.* But is

113

it? He lived a life of parties with lots of drinking and girls. He spent his money trying to be a popular fellow everyone would like. Finally, he ran out of money. Times got hard, and no one helped him. His so-called friends disappeared, he was alone and impoverished, and he ended up with a menial job feeding pigs. He didn't feel so happy and free anymore.

When he came to his senses, he thought about the home he left. Dying with hunger and realizing he had wasted his life with loose living, he decided to go home, thinking he could at least be hired by his father as a farm hand. First, he had to figure out what he would say to his father. (This is important. When we are in situations involving forgiveness, it's a good idea to plan what we need to say and how to say it. It would be good to address the person we sinned against, tell exactly what we did wrong, perhaps adding a statement of how we have hurt or affected them, and then use the words, "Will you forgive me?") This young man decided to say, "Father, I have sinned against heaven and in your sight; I am no longer worthy to be called your son; make me as one of your hired men" (Luke 15:18-19). He was surprised when his father, who had seen him coming, ran out to meet him. The father quickly ordered his servants to prepare a party in honor of his homecoming. He said that they must celebrate, "For this son of mine was dead, and has come to life again; he was lost and has been found" (Luke 15:24).

If the father in the story represents God, many of us can identify with this lost son. We fail to realize how much the heavenly Father loves us and longs for us to be one with him. We go away from him because we are ignorant of what life is really all about, and we want to live it our way. At some point we may hit hard times and realize something is missing. If we are fortunate enough to come to our senses and knowledgeable enough to try God as our answer, we may be surprised by his love and acceptance, by the wonderful life he enables us to live and enjoy, and by how much his love transforms us into a new person.

The other son in this story stayed home with his father, but he too never realized the love of the father. When he saw how his father treated his wayward brother, he was angry and would not join the welcome home celebration. His father pleaded with him to come join them, but he would not. He criticized his father for never giving him a party so he could celebrate with his friends. His father tried to explain things, but his son would not listen. Instead, he resented his father's actions and would not accept his brother back. Obviously, this son also needed to learn what love and forgiveness was all about. Without love, we don't forgive, and without forgiveness, we miss out on loving relationships and a better life.

Sometimes I wonder how many of us say we believe in God as our Father but never practice what the Father says to do—to love and forgive as a way of life. The Bible is right when it says we love because God first loved us (1 John 4:19). I'm guessing that the first son in this story, because he experienced his father's love, became a lover of others. The second son never entered into the depths of his father's love and therefore remained only able to get along with people he liked and who liked him. Others needed to be accepted and loved by him, but that he could not do.

The power of being accepted and loved is evident in many of life's interactions. The spirit of forgiveness can be conveyed to people when this attitude of acceptance and love toward them is in us. I have seen people who have felt judged, mistreated, and rejected, changed for the better when they are in the presence of people who accept them and patiently love them. When we experience love and acceptance through God's forgiveness, it changes us and puts in us that kind of a spirit we can give to others. The father in the previous story accepted and loved his sons almost as if they had already been forgiven before they experienced it. When the first son was loved and forgiven and accepted by his father, he probably acquired that spirit within himself and could convey it to others. The second son who would not humble himself and be forgiving had not experienced it from his father, as is evident by not being able to give it to his brother.

A friend of mine shared this illustration with me on the power of love and acceptance toward others: Every day a man would come and leave his car parked in front of his and his wife's house. They did not want him parking there because they often had visitors to their home and needed the space for guests to park, especially if a visitor needed help into the house. My friend wrote a note to him and left it on his car. The note explained their situation and asked if he could please park farther up the street. But the man kept parking there. My friend prayed about it, relied on God for wisdom, and wrote another note. This time he apologized to the man for asking him to move, saying that he had a right to the street, even as everyone else, and that if he wanted to stay there, he would understand. The next day, and thereafter, the man parked elsewhere. In the first note, the man could easily have felt judged and not accepted for who he was. He rebelled against doing what was asked of him. The second note conveyed acceptance for who he was and gave him permission to be himself. The power of that approach was evident. Love, acceptance, and forgiveness, when experienced from God, gives us an inner spirit or attitude of love and forgiveness toward others, makes a difference in how we treat them, and can have a transforming affect in their lives.

We are often afraid to show love and respect for others because we think we will be agreeing with their wrong attitudes and behaviors. We think accepting them lets them think they are all right the way they are and that they don't need to change. That is not true. What it does is draw them into a relationship with you, and if you are a follower of Christ, you then have opportunity to let them see God in your life, and you can be an influence to help them also want to believe in the God of love. We can't change people, but God's grace can, and his love in us can point them in that direction.

LOVE, FORGIVENESS, AND JUDGING OTHERS

An example of how God's forgiveness makes us more loving was explained by Jesus in a story he told to a judgmental person who looked down on others (Luke 7:36-50). Jesus told the judgmental person about a man who graciously forgave the debt owed to him by two people. One owed him a lot of money, the other owed little, but neither one had the means to repay. They were both forgiven their debts. Jesus asked the judgmental person, "Which one of them will love him more?" The man answered, "I suppose the one whom he forgave more." Jesus said, "You have judged correctly."

Then Jesus mentioned a sinful woman in the room who was showing love to Jesus. The judgmental man could not understand

116

how Jesus could accept such a woman who deserved judgment for her sins. Jesus said to the judgmental person, "Do you see this woman?" He then explained to the man how this sinful woman showed more love to him than the judgmental person did, and he told why. Jesus said, "I say to you, her sins, which were many, have been forgiven, for she showed much love; but he who is forgiven little, loves little." In other words, the more we feel forgiven by God, the greater our love for others will be. Those without God's forgiveness love little. What Jesus was trying to point out to the man was that he needed God's forgiveness in his life for his judgmentalism, just like the second son in the previous story we just examined. Without true forgiveness, we remain self-focused, and we love little.

Many point to a statement Jesus once made about not judging people. He said, "Do not judge, lest you be judged" (Matthew 7:1). They like to use Jesus' statement to say to others, "Don't judge me. Let me be who I am, and accept me for who I am." They think Jesus is teaching us not to make judgments about people. They ignore another statement Jesus made about judging people. He said, "Do not judge according to appearance, but judge with righteous judgment" (John 7:24). Parents believe in this principle when they tell their children not to hang around with such and such a person because of their bad influence. We need to make judgments about people to avoid evil that could be inflicted on us by them.

I was once sexually abused by a man, and when it happened, I judged him as a bad person who I did not want to be around, and I avoided him thereafter. Without such a judgment, I could have put myself in danger of further abuse that might easily have led to becoming a really messed up person. Judging another person does not mean we cannot or will not accept them, but it does mean we need to make right judgments about the kind of involvement we need to allow or not allow.

When we have a true sense of God's right and wrong, it is natural to recoil when in the presence of evil and to avoid it for the sake of our well-being. Discerning good from evil is an important judgment to make in a world like ours. But learning how to love and accept people also has its proper place. God's Word and Spirit in us will teach us when and how to be involved and when to run.

Not judging people, and expressing love and acceptance, while at the same time making righteous judgments, depends on our growth in Christ-like character and the strength we have for resisting evil. The man who molested me eventually asked my forgiveness, and I forgave him. Although we were never friends, it was healing. I understand that young children taken advantage of do not have the power to resist abuse as was true in my case. It is very sad, and they will need special attention to help them overcome what it does to them.

CLOSING REMARKS

To close the chapter, I need to point out three things. (1) I promised in the beginning of this chapter to share a book that has helped me learn lots about forgiveness. Check the footnote.[7] (2) Forgiveness does not mean we can do what we want if it feels good, while knowing it is wrong, and take advantage of our belief that God will forgive us. The Apostle Paul makes this point by saying, "Are we to continue in sin so that grace may increase? May it never be! How shall we who died to sin still live in it?" (Romans 6:1-2). When we are forgiven, we no longer want to be like we were. We strive, with God's help, to be holy and perfect as God is holy and perfect (Matthew 5:48; 1 Peter 1:14-16). We may not be able to achieve perfection in this life, but as God's forgiven people, and because we love him, we want it, and we work toward it. (3) On the other hand, if we commit a sin, we confess it, believe God's forgiveness, and know that "there is now no condemnation for those who are in Christ Jesus" (see 1 John 1:5-2:2; Romans 8:1). Guilt does not need to rule your life.

Sometimes people have a problem with feeling forgiven. I will tell you about a common experience I had that many people have. It's the problem of doing the same sin over and over and not being able to change—or another problem some people have is not *wanting* to change. Every time I did the same sin again and again and again, which I did not like and didn't seem able to change, I would confess to God, repent, and ask forgiveness. Then I would believe God forgave me. After doing this for quite a long time, I started to question, *How*

---

7. Frank Desiderio, CSP, *Can You Let Go of a Grudge? Learn to Forgive and Get On with Your Life* (Mahwah, NJ: Paulist Press, 2014).

can God keep forgiving me when I keep doing this? But I knew he did forgive me because Jesus died for my sin, and the Bible said, "There is now no condemnation for those who are in Christ Jesus." The Bible says I am free from the law of sin and death (Romans 8:1-2).

I knew I was forgiven and would still go to heaven, but one day, doubt crept in, and after sinning again, I had these thoughts: *God, how can you keep forgiving me? I keep doing wrong, and I can't believe you keep forgiving me, but you do. You do keep forgiving me.* I felt terribly unworthy of his forgiveness. I could have gotten down on myself for being a failure, given in to my guilt feelings, and given up and quit trying to change, thinking I will never change. I could have despaired, thinking God at some point would stop forgiving me. But I didn't let that happen. At this point, I did not let doubt take over my life. I affirmed God's truth and was amazed that God kept forgiving me. I was amazed at how much he loved me to keep doing that without fail.

Suddenly I had the thought, *I can't keep doing this. I can't keep letting God down. I have to do something to stop sinning and be the person God wants me to be.* His forgiving love made me realize that I didn't want to keep sinning, and I was now more serious about working at changing. I said, *God, help me not be this way anymore.* I had said that before, but seeing how God kept loving me now broke my heart at how I was disappointing him, and I had greater motivation to want to change when I realized how much he loved me. I didn't want to keep taking God's forgiveness for granted.

Wanting to change had nothing to do with a fear of whether God would keep forgiving me or not; I knew he always forgives me because Jesus took my sin and my punishment for me. I realized I did not have to fear God's judgment. The Bible says, "We have come to know and have believed the love which God has for us. . . . By this, love is perfected with us so that we may have confidence in the day of judgment. . . . There is no fear in love; but perfect love casts out fear, because fear involves punishment, and the one who fears is not perfected in love" (1 John 4:16-18). I did not have to change anything about myself to be loved, forgiven, and accepted by God, and I had no fear of his judgment. But I did have to change to have a good relationship with God.

119

That day, believing I am forgiven and realizing how much he loved me to keep forgiving me motivated me to resolve to change. The change did not happen overnight, but I no longer wanted sin in my life, and God helped me change. The key is to never give up believing you are forgiven by God. I think that one day it gets to you, and all of a sudden you don't want to be that way anymore, and you make a plan to follow Jesus and live as he wants. I do this not to be accepted by him—for he already accepts us—but for the sake of knowing I am pleasing my heavenly Father as his beloved child.

Referring again to Romans 6:1-2, I paraphrase this question and answer, *Shall we keep sinning because we know God forgives us? May it never be. How shall we who died to sin still live in it?* Romans 6–8 are some of the best parts of the Bible to help us want to overcome sin in our lives. I will never be sinless in this life, but I know God loves and forgives me, and I want to become more like Jesus in how I live my life. There is no pressure or fear of God not loving and liking me. I have discovered that God is patient and gentle with me as he helps me live for him. Therefore, every time you sin, thank God for forgiving you, and tell him you want and need him to help you change. He knows your heart. You are his beloved child (1 John 3:1-3). But, if I truly respect God, his love, and his holiness, I will not want to keep hurting his heart and will become very serious about doing all I can to change.

CHAPTER 7

UNDERSTANDING GOD'S LOVE AND THE CROSS OF JESUS

As an aide and a teacher in our town's high school, my wife received graduation invitations from many students. As a graduation gift she gave nice-looking crosses on silver chains. The students all seemed to appreciate them. One day, driving back from a long trip, I stopped at a gas station and convenience store one hundred fifty miles from home. The bus transporting our hometown baseball team had also stopped there. I recognized one of the players, and I was surprised to see him wearing the cross necklace from my wife. When I greeted him and commented about it, he said he never takes it off.

Many people wear crosses as jewelry pieces. Jesus' cross must carry a lot of meaning for it to be such popular decor. What is it that attracts people to the cross? Do they consider the cross to be a good luck charm, a symbol of their faith, a divine means of protection from harm? What? I doubt very much that people in ancient Rome wore crosses. Crosses were implementations used for the cruel execution of criminals. If you or I had been there when Jesus was crucified, we might have thought, *There's another person being executed for his crimes.* Or, if we had known about Jesus or had experienced his goodness, we might have wondered, *What must that good man have done to end up on a Roman cross?* There is no way that by simply observing Jesus' death on the cross we would know what it meant. That is why we must rely on the biblical words written by his informed disciples, apostles, and Old Testament prophets, to discover the meaning of the cross.

Jesus was not a criminal, evildoer, or traitor against Rome. He never did anything wrong and did not deserve to die on a Roman cross. Why then was he there? Humanly speaking, he was there because he was unjustly accused of wrongs, hated by jealous people who feared his rise to popularity and power, was thought to be an impostor and blasphemer for claiming to be the Son of God and the promised Messiah, and was accused of being a troublemaker and threat to peace in the surrounding region. He was pronounced innocent by his Roman judge (John 19:4), but the judge permitted his execution to save his own position of power, fearing that if he let Jesus go, a riot could erupt. His trial and execution were unjust from start to finish. Jesus said that he could be delivered from all of this (Matthew 26:53-54), but he accepted his death as the will of his Father in heaven (Luke 22:42; John 10:17-18; 12:27). His death had a divine purpose.

PEOPLE RECOGNIZE THE NEED FOR LOVE AND JUSTICE

We already know that the world needs more love. It is the absence of love that causes the need for justice. I have in mind two kinds of justice: social justice and criminal justice. Social justice is needed when people are suffering from sicknesses, famine, war, devastating storms, being economically poor, lack of basic needs like water or housing, or ill treatment by others—for example, prejudice and discrimination, such as racism or being shunned as outcasts. People's hearts go out to those who suffer such disasters or ill-treatment, and good people want to do something about it. If people see those who are poor and starving or lacking in other basic needs, they reach out to help them. People who rally together with upheld signs and raised voices, demonstrating for certain causes on the streets of our cities, want to see changes made to correct things they believe are not right. Domestic violence and abuses in homes is a recognized condition that we say must not be tolerated. To make their world a better place, most people have things bothering them that they would like to see changed or eliminated. The above feelings and actions show that people have an inner sense that bad situations need to be made good, and wrong situations need to be made right. In people's minds, these social concerns ought to be resolved. God has the same concern.

Criminal justice is the second kind of justice. If people have a crime committed against them, they get angry and want to see those committing the crime caught and punished and restitution made. Humans often get away with immoral behaviors and terrible crimes, and their victims suffer from wrongs that are never made right. If crime against them is not resolved, people get the feeling that life is not fair and is not as it ought to be. It bothers people to see so much injustice in the world. We humans may differ over what is good or bad, right or wrong; nevertheless, we all possess a basic moral compass of good and bad, right and wrong. Every person seems to want what they believe is good and right to triumph over what's bad and wrong. God has the same concern—he cares that justice is done.

Although humans see the need for love and justice, and they have a vision of a harmonious and peaceful world, they have never been able to make it happen. They try to make a harmonious and peaceful world through voluntary individual or group projects designed to meet people's unmet needs. They try to make a harmonious and peaceful world happen through government systems of law and order. Some try to make a harmonious and peaceful world by taking matters into their own hands, thinking it is their right or duty to correct wrong situations. If enough people are dissatisfied with how things are, sadly, they try to make a harmonious and peaceful world through war. People also try to make a harmonious and peaceful world through the practice of religion. The truth is that there are always evils preventing the kind of world people want. What hope is there for the loving, peaceful, righteous, and happy world that most people crave? People do not have the power or ability to bring about the kind of world they hope for.

Besides well-meaning human projects, government systems, taking matters into one's own hands, war, and religions, is there any other way to bring about a world of love and peace? One day, history records that a man named Jesus was born into the world. Those who have taken serious notice of him have observed that his words and deeds give hope for such a world. When Jesus was on earth, he went about doing good and correcting all sorts of wrongful conditions. This included feeding the poor, healing the sick, calming storms, raising the dead, transforming people's lives, and so forth. He spoke of a God different from all the other gods people worship. Jesus said his words, and power came from that God, and he demonstrated what a good world would be like if God's love and power was in charge. Knowing that love is missing and that justice is often unfair or left undone in this world, many people believe that to make all things right, there is need for someone with greater power than humans. Jesus implied that people's defiled hearts are a problem for the world being the way it is (Mark 7:14-23). So how can God change human hearts and bring about the kind of loving world people want? The cross of Jesus is God's way to do it.

UNDERSTANDING THE MEANING OF THE CROSS OF JESUS

Do you agree with the need for love and justice in our world? Can you think of anyone who has done something wrong to you that made you angry? Did you feel that the wrong needed to be made right? What quiets your anger at the person or persons who wronged you? Do you feel better if the guilty person is made to pay for his crime against you and if compensation is made for your losses? Love cares to make wrong things right. The proper action taken to make wrong things right is what *justice* is all about. God's own Son, Jesus, who he sent to love and help people, was mocked, spit upon,

124

and rejected, and unjustly suffered a cruel death. God has suffered injustice because of people's crimes against him. God knows how we feel when justice is not done. The wrongs must be made right.

It is right for God to be appropriately angry at wrong things; they are not the way he intended them to be, and they hurt people. Everyone who has done or is doing wrong is subject to God's anger and wrath. All who are guilty must be punished. Those who have wronged God must be punished. The truth is, we are all guilty and deserving of his judgment (Romans 1:18; 3:23; Ephesians 2:1-3). It would not be right for God to forgo justice, for God cannot look with favor on wrongdoers (Habakkuk 1:13; Psalm 130:3; Revelation 6:15-17). God is slow to anger and does not want this for people (Ezekiel 18:23, 32), but if wrong and unrepentance continues after many unheeded warnings, he is bound by his holiness and love to punish the wrongdoers. God must exercise justice on two fronts: justice for all who have wronged him and justice on earth for all people who suffer the wrongs of others.

The cross of Jesus is not just for us, it is also for God. He wants to save people, along with the heavens and the earth, which he created to be our home. Both God and people must rely on the cross of Jesus to make God's salvation possible. Because of God's holy hatred and wrath against the evils of wrongdoing, his justice requires that he must judge and punish the wrongdoers by condemning them to death. To save us, God must rely on Jesus, the Son of God, to make it right for him to forgive people for the wrongs they have committed against him. Because humans are under the penalty of death, humans must rely on Jesus, the Son of man, to make it possible for them to be forgiven and freed from their sin against God and their just condemnation to death. Thus the Son of God, by his death on the cross, makes it possible for God to love and forgive; and the Son of man, by his death on the cross, makes it possible for humankind to be loved and forgiven.

What does condemnation to death mean? The Bible says that "the wages of sin is death, but the gracious gift of God is eternal life" (Romans 6:23). God warned humans in the beginning that choosing evil would result in death (Genesis 2:17). We could say that physical death is a part of the penalty we pay for our sinning, but there is an ultimate sentence of death that God pronounces. This is labeled a second death (Revelation 21:8). The second death is not a physical death, for all who die are raised to life again, both the righteous and the unrighteous (John 5:28-29; Revelation 20:4-6, 11-15). This sentence of a second death from God means being sentenced to separation from God and from life in his kingdom. Why this ultimate sentence of death? Because no evil can be permitted within God's holy being nor within his eternal realm (Psalm 5:4). God's plan is to create a new world of perfect righteousness and to bring people into this new world (Matthew 28:19-20; 2 Peter 3:13). He cannot do it, however, without the cross of Jesus and its benefit of restoring God's kind of life to all who believe.

Sadly, there are those who continually reject God, and it is because of their failure to receive his offer of salvation that he must sentence them to a life of separation from his righteous kingdom (John 3:36). They choose to remain the way they are instead of allowing God to make them into new creations in Christ who are freed from the penalty of sin and death.

We have just said that for humans to be saved requires what Jesus did on the cross, and for God to save, also requires what Jesus did on the cross. We need the cross so we can be forgiven, made righteous, and be raised from the dead to eternal life. The Bible says, "If we confess our sins, he is faithful and righteous to forgive us our sins and to cleanse us from all unrighteousness" (1 John 1:9). Notice that God is faithful *and righteous* to forgive. God relies on the cross to satisfy his justice and make it right for him to be merciful and forgive us. God must be able to do what human judges cannot do. If a human judge says to a guilty lawbreaker, "I forgive you, go and be free," he is not being just if the guilty is set free instead of being punished. The victims of the crime will cry out that justice has not been done. The judge may want to forgive but must punish wrongdoing. So how can God do both? He does it by sending Jesus on his behalf to pay the penalty for the wrongdoer's crimes. This means that Jesus takes God's punishment in place of the person who committed the crime so that the criminal can be forgiven. Jesus, motivated by God's love for us, voluntarily offered himself to God as payment for our wrongs. Jesus took away the reason for God's anger against us by taking on himself the penalty of death that we deserved (Romans 5:8-10). There is now no condemnation to those who are in Christ Jesus (Romans 8:1).

A question that puzzles some people is this: *How can someone take another person's punishment?* To us, it doesn't make sense because in our justice system, people must pay for their own crimes or wrongs. The judge must follow the law and punish the wrongdoer (Romans 13:1-4). One day Jesus talked about how impossible it is for a rich person to be saved, and those who heard this asked him, "Then who can be saved?" Jesus replied, "The things that are impossible with people are possible with God" (Luke 18:17-27). Humans can never perform what God says is needed to be saved; therefore, no one can save him or herself. But God can. Even though it is a mystery to us, God makes his way clear, and there is nothing we can do but believe that his way of salvation works. When a man asked the Apostle Paul what he must do to be saved, Paul answered, "Believe in the Lord Jesus, and you will be saved" (Acts 16:30-31). The message of the cross seems foolish to people, but if they believe it, it works as the power of God to save them (1 Corinthians 1:18).

There is also something about Jesus' taking other people's punishment on the cross that changes their hearts so that they no longer want to live as they have been living. Jesus giving up his life on the cross provides a motivation that leads some people to want to live a new way, and it leads them to accept God's offer of a new life. The cross becomes an act of God's love, softening a person's heart, that together with God's Spirit at work, enables a change in those who believe. The cross of Jesus makes true salvation happen for the forgiven person because it does not leave the recipient unchanged; rather, the recipient becomes a new creation who acquires God's righteousness, thus fitting him or her to live in the kingdom of God (Philippians 3:8-11).

How does Christ giving up his life for others impact people and motivate them to want to change their lives? Here are two stories about punishing wrongdoers that can perhaps help us better understand how God's method of the cross helps to change the wrongdoer. The first story involves Amos Bronson Alcott (1799–1888), an American philosopher and teacher who, in his day, wanted to reform the way they educated children. When it came to punishing children in school for their misdeeds, he saw wrong thoughts in their minds as the reason for their misbehavior. Therefore, his method of punishment was designed to help change their minds about what they did. Instead of punishing a student for his wrongdoing, he would take the student's punishment on himself by having the student hit him across the knuckles with a stick or ruler. Surprisingly, this idea of the innocent suffering in place of the guilty proved to be effective. Students did not like the idea of hitting their teacher, and not wanting to be the cause of pain in someone else, this strange method of punishment helped curb school misbehaviors. Somehow, it deeply affects people to see the innocent suffer for the guilty. Personally, it helps me want to change my bad behavior when I see what my wrongdoing did to Jesus.

The second story is about a son who related what hurt him the most when punished by his father. He said that it wasn't the lecture his father gave him about what he had done wrong, nor was it the spanking he got. He knew he deserved the punishment he was getting. What affected him the most was that his dad would break down in tears during the punishment of his son. It made him feel sorry that the wrong he had done had so deeply hurt his father. When reading the Bible, one of the problems people have concerning God is that when they see him punish people for their sins, they see him as mean and not loving. One reason is because they fail to see his tears (for example, Luke 19:41-44). God's punishment must be given according to the nature of the wrong, but when it is done with compassion, love, and tears, it is not seen as a mean act but as an act of love to help a person want to change and become better. Also, when God knows that a person is beyond willingness to repent and change (Proverbs 29:1; 2 Chronicles 36:11-16), it grieves him that by rejecting his compassion and warnings, they put themselves beyond remedy (Genesis 6:5-6).

WORDS IN THE BIBLE EXPLAINING WHAT JESUS DID

There is a word in the Bible that helps explain what Jesus did to meet God's need for justice and our need to be forgiven. That word is often translated as "propitiation," or "atoning sacrifice," or "reconciliation," and it means that Jesus, out of love, voluntarily sacrificed himself to satisfy the justice of God, thus allowing God to be favorable toward us (see Romans 3:23-26; Hebrews 2:17; 1 John 2:1-2; 4:9-10). It means Jesus took God's wrath upon himself, suffering the death that should have been ours (John 3:36) so our relationship with God could be restored (1 Peter 2:24; Isaiah 53:4-6). Through faith in Christ Jesus, we are saved from God's wrath and are now at peace with God (Romans 5:1, 9; 1 Thessalonians 5:9-10). His death has *reconciled* God to us and us to God (2 Corinthians 5:18-21). Think of a clock that tells the wrong time. When set to the right time by using another clock, the wrong clock is reconciled to the correct clock. Through Jesus, we are reconciled with God so we can be in true harmony with him and his will for us (Romans 5:10-11; Colossians 1:19-20).

There are other words in the Bible, besides *propitiation*, *atonement*, and *reconciliation*, to help explain the meaning of Jesus' death on the cross. The cross allows God to justify a person. *Justified* means we are declared not guilty, and by our faith in Jesus, God credits us as righteous (Romans 4:1-16; 3:19-28; 5:1). The cross is a *ransom* payment, a price paid to release someone from bondage or captivity—to set him or her free. Christ died on the cross to pay a ransom for people who are in slavery (Matthew 20:28; 1 Timothy 2:5-6).

Who or what enslaves us? We can say the devil and his influence has a hold over us (Hebrews 2:14-15). We can also say our sins enslave us (John 8:34-36). Since God is the one who frees us, perhaps we can say that the ransom payment is made by Jesus to God the Father who releases us from slavery to sin and death. The cross is a means of *redemption* (Colossians 1:13-14; Galatians 3:13; 4:4-5; Romans 8:23; Ephesians 1:7; Psalm 107:1-2). Redemption means to buy something back so as to regain ownership (1 Corinthians 6:19-20; 7:23; Acts 20:28). I remember hearing the story of a boy who lost his toy boat when the waves took it out into deeper water, and he couldn't get it back. Weeks later, he noticed his boat in a store window. He went in to get it back, but the owner told him he had to pay. When he paid, he redeemed his boat; he owned it again. God lost us when we went away from him. Jesus paid the price of redemption so that we could again belong to God. Jesus, as the only sinless human, is a sacrifice that God will accept. As such, he is the only one who can save us—there is no other savior (Acts 4:12; John 3:16-18). This is why Paul preached Jesus Christ and him crucified (1 Corinthians 1:23-24; 2:2, 5).

APPLYING JESUS' DEATH TO OUR LIVES

During my twenty years of doing Fifth Steps at an alcohol and drug treatment center, I heard numerous stories from broken people whose tragic lives became ruined by their life-dominating and corrupting habits. Most of them were actually thankful for their destructive past when they realized that it brought them to this treatment center where they were discovering a better way to live. One woman shared with me all the details of wasting her life in drunken stupor, ending up alone, losing everything, and desperate for freedom from her life-destroying addictions. Near the end of her treatment, she admitted to being deeply bothered by guilty feelings over how she had hurt the people she loved. Guilt was a common problem among many individuals in the program. Although group therapy helped them feel better about themselves, it did not rid them of the gnawing conscience and deep guilt that remained on the backburner of their minds.

When the woman I was talking to finished her story and said she still felt guilty, I asked her if she would like to hear God's solution for guilt. She answered, "Yes." Over the years, I asked that question to many in treatment who admitted they could not overcome their guilty feelings, and all but one wanted to hear God's solution. I said it a little differently to each person as I tried to relate to each one's situation. When I explained God's solution for guilt to this woman, her face lit up, and she believed it, experienced forgiveness, grew in her faith over the years, has remained a changed person, and has shared with me how relationships with many in her family have been restored.

Many in life have no clue about the significance of Jesus being called the Lamb of God. Jesus is called "the Lamb of God who takes away the sin of the world" (John 1:29). A picture of Jesus as a lamb and what this means is given us in Genesis 22 where Abraham builds an altar and is going to offer up his son as a sacrifice on a mountain where God directed him to go. His son, asks, "Where is the lamb for the burnt offering?" and Abraham simply replies to him, "God will provide for himself the lamb for the burnt offering." As Abraham is about to kill his own son, God's voice interrupts, and a ram appears that is caught in a nearby thicket. Abraham takes the ram and sacrifices it in the place of his son. Abraham calls the place, "The Lord Will Provide," and it became a saying: "In the mount of the Lord it will be provided."

Likewise, the cross of Jesus is the place where God provided a Lamb to take the place of the guilty. I have an idea that Abraham's incident that took place on one of the hills at the Moriah location is where Jesus would one day die as God's lamb (compare Genesis 22:2 with 2 Chronicles 3:1).

There is an inclination in all of us to cover up our guilt. It is easy to excuse our wrongs by justifying what we did or by blaming others. People will say, "It's OK, everyone does wrong, it only shows we're human," or they excuse themselves by saying, "I am not the only one at fault in the situation—I blame them for [whatever]." NO! We all need to own our guilt. Unless it is a thought or act we should not feel guilty about, most guilt feelings mean we are guilty. Admit it: we are all guilty and deserving of whatever consequences result from our actions. King David of ancient Israel said to God, "I have sinned and done what is evil in your sight, so that you are justified when you speak and blameless when you judge" (Psalm 51:2-4). He owned his guilt and accepted whatever just payment he deserved for what he did. Part of our responsibility to be forgiven is to honestly agree with God about the wrongs we have done and what we deserve. We need not fear admitting our sin and facing God's condemnation, for in the death of Christ Jesus, God provided a way to escape it.

The Bible records other historical events that help us get a picture of the purpose Christ accomplished on the cross. The Passover story is a good example (Exodus 12:21-27). God's people were slaves and oppressed by the Egyptians. As a just judgment for their evil ways, and to convince Egypt's king to set his people free, God sent an angel of death to kill the firstborn in every Egyptian home. He told the Israelites how to protect themselves from this sentence of death. They were to kill a lamb and put its blood on the door frame of their houses. When the angel of death came, he would see the blood and pass over the houses without harming those inside (Exodus 12:12-

13). The Israelites were spared by believing God's warning. Likewise, when by faith we apply the blood of Jesus to our lives, death will pass over us, and we will never die. The Bible says that Jesus is our Passover (1 Corinthians 5:7).

The serpent on the pole is another story illustrating how the cross heals our souls (Numbers 21:6-9). Unbelieving Israelites were suffering sickness and death as judgment for their sins, and they cried out for Moses to pray and ask God to save them. God told Moses to make a pole with a serpent on it, and if anyone looked at the pole, thus exercising faith in God's word of promise, he or she would be healed. Jesus applied this event to himself as the one lifted up on a pole—the cross—and if people will gaze upon him and believe, he will heal them of their sin and death (John 3:14-15).

God is holy. All evil and unrighteousness is repulsive to God. When Jesus died on a cross and took our sins in his body on the cross (1 Peter 2:24), he was repulsive to God. Perhaps that is why he said, "My God, my God, why have you forsaken me?" (Mark 15:34). In a lesser measure, we feel the same as God toward evil and wrongs—we are also repulsed by them. I once began to read a book about how another race of people were being treated, even tortured, by evil people. I had to get rid of the book as I felt sickened and could not believe how horrendously evil humans could be to other humans. There are many behaviors that are repulsive to us, and they should be because we are created in God's image and thus have a similar nature to his—one that has a hatred of evil and wrongdoing, especially when we experience what it does to us. God does not like it, and he cannot allow it to continue without correction or elimination. God is our ultimate judge (Hebrews 9:27; 2 Corinthians 5:10; Acts 17:30-31; Revelation 20:12; Ecclesiastes 12:14). He must exercise perfect justice and has no recourse but to judge what people are guilty of doing and to give out proper retribution for what each has done. In the case of the cross, Jesus suffered rejection from God, a rejection we would have had to endure if he had not died.

God is also a God of mercy (Ephesians 2:4-5). He would prefer to see us freed from our wrongdoing, guilt, and death (Romans 6:23; Ezekiel 18:23, 32; 2 Peter 3:9). Here is where the cross of Christ Jesus comes into significance, for at the cross, justice and mercy are accomplished at the same time. Think about the story of your life. It includes every ugly and disgusting thought you've ever had and every prideful, selfish, immoral, shameful, destructive, and hurtful thing you've ever done to yourself and others—things you may not want anyone else to know. Jesus lived a perfect life, and there is no sin in him. Your life of wrongdoing is unacceptable to God, but God has nothing against his Son. There is no reason for God to punish him, no reason for him to die because of his sins (because he had none). You are invited to give Jesus all your wrongs, and they are all on him. What does he do with them? He allows himself to suffer an extremely cruel, undeserved, painful death on a cross for all you and I have ever done against God, self, and others. On the cross, Jesus is taking God's anger, wrath, and punishment on himself, not for his sins but for yours and mine. Because you have given your sins to God, there is no more sin in your life; it is gone. You are free, and God accepts you as if you had never done anything wrong. Furthermore, Christ has given you something in return for you giving him your wrongs. He gives you his righteousness and the status as a child of God. He has made it possible for God to declare you "not guilty," and by the power of his Holy Spirit, he gives you a new heart, equipping you to enjoy a new life that death can no longer destroy (John 11:25-26). In Christ's death on the cross, God's justice and mercy has been accomplished on your behalf.

THE CROSS OF JESUS AS AN EXAMPLE

We must not neglect another meaning of the cross. Jesus' death on the cross is an example for us on how to live that new life he has given us. He gives us his example of dying. Jesus not only died physically, he died to his self-will in order to live for the will of his Father in heaven. All who follow him are characterized by the same heart: to do the Father's will. This is what he said is true about his followers—they are "whoever does the will of My Father who is in heaven" (Matthew 12:50). That is why he gave us his Holy Spirit when we believed, to motivate and empower us to die to ourselves and to live for God (Romans 6:10-11; Ephesians 4:22-24). Following are two particular examples that Jesus modeled for us by his death on the cross.

First, his death is an example of his love. He wants us to love others as he has loved us. He said, "Greater love has no one than

133

this, that one lay down his life for his friends" (John 15:13). He does not necessarily mean to die physically for others. But, as he died to self-will for the good of others, we are willing to die to our self-will and live for the good and well-being of others. His love through us extends to everyone: love your fellow believers (John 13:34-35), love your neighbor as yourself (Luke 10:27), love your wife (Ephesians 5:25), love the world of people (John 3:16), love even your enemies (Matthew 5:43-48).

The second example Jesus gave in dying on the cross was bearing up under the sorrows of suffering unjustly. When we suffer for doing what is right and patiently endure it, this finds favor with God. When Jesus was mistreated, he did not threaten back but entrusted himself to God to righteously judge his enemies for how they unfairly treated him (1 Peter 2:19-23). There are times we need to respond in this way. Joseph in the Old Testament was a good example when he was sold into slavery by his brothers and later spent time in prison for being falsely accused of wrongdoing.

QUESTIONS TO ANSWER

The questions for you (and me) are these: Have you understood and believed the meaning of "Christ died for our sins?" (1 Corinthians 15:1-4). Have you admitted your sin and agreed with God that you are guilty and that God is righteous to place you under the sentence of death? Has what he did for you, because you are believing it, freed you from all your guilt and shame, from all your self-condemnation, and from thinking you are not a good person? By seeing, believing, trusting, and receiving by faith the person of Jesus, are you sure that God has forgiven you and that you now possess the hope of a future in his kingdom of peace, love, joy, and freedom from all evil? Are you experiencing the joy of being free? Do you feel clean, like a new person having a new start in life? Has God's love through Christ Jesus given you a heart of love for him that is motivating you to change your life and live differently than you did before?

CHAPTER 8

GOD'S PROVIDENTIAL LOVE

I n this chapter I write about the good things God does for people and also why God would allow people to go through bad things. Both are demonstrations that he loves and cares for us.

One of the great promises God wants us to believe without fail is that God is with us. The name of a child to be born at a future time was prophesied in Isaiah 7:14. When Jesus was born, that prophecy was fulfilled, and that name was given to Jesus. He is *Immanuel,* which means "God with us" (Matthew 1:23). All the good he did for others, the meaning of his death, and his resurrection, was living proof that God is indeed with us (John 1:1-3, 14).

In Genesis, God promised to be with Jacob and bless the whole world through his descendants (Genesis 28:13-21). When Jacob's son, Joseph, was betrayed by his brothers, taken and sold in Egypt as a slave, and imprisoned for over two years for something he did not do, God was with him and was helping him prosper in all that happened (Genesis 39). He later became second in command over all of Egypt, and God used him to save many people alive, including all of Egypt, his family, and the brothers who betrayed him. *God with us* means that he will work all things, even bad things, for good (Romans 8:28).

David, a shepherd boy, and later a king of Israel, wrote this: "Even though I walk through the valley of the shadow of death, I fear no evil, for You are with me; Your rod and Your staff, they comfort me. . . . Surely goodness and lovingkindness will follow me all the days of my life, and I will dwell in the house of the Lord forever" (Psalm 23:4, 6). The promise of *God with him* gave him peace, comfort, and the hope that all would end well, even in the midst of fearful and evil circumstances. The New Testament also reminds us of God's promise: "I will never desert you, nor will I ever forsake you" (Hebrews 13:5).

One of the proofs that God is with us is seeing the providential events that he causes to happen in our daily lives. For example, when I was a boy about eleven years of age, I was sitting on my bike in front of my house, watching kids play. My dog was on the enclosed front porch barking, wanting out to join all the excitement. He kept barking, so I finally got off my bike and went to the porch door to let the dog out. As soon as I touched the handle on the door, I heard a loud noise and turned around. A heavy branch from a large tree had broken off and crashed down on the bike where I was sitting. I don't know what injury I might have been spared. Later on, I realized this as an act of God's goodness.

Have you ever had things happen and thought, *That was lucky how that worked out*, or, *What was the chance of that happening?* or, *I can't believe I wasn't killed; someone upstairs must have been looking out for me.* I have not interviewed people about this, but I would venture to guess that most people could think of something that turned out good in their life, something unexpected that seemed like it was caused by a mysterious power. Perhaps you've had a feeling like something greater, perhaps a universal force, destiny, or someone other than yourself was at work in your life. As I thought back over my life, I made a list of over thirty events, showing me that God was with me and cared about me.

Once, my eighteen-year-old daughter and I were going on a short-term mission trip to Colombia, South America, to help with a much-needed building project. We had a garage sale in our driveway to raise a little money for the trip. When the sale had ended, I sat in the driveway and counted up the money: $199.50. I mentioned to God, *If we had fifty cents more, we would have two hundred dollars even.* Just then, a young boy appeared from around the corner of the house and began looking around at all the stuff. He asked if he could buy something. I asked, "How much do you have?" He said, "Fifty cents." I said, "You can have anything here for fifty cents."

Here is one more story. My wife and I retired from our work and were leaving to go back east where our kids and grandkids lived. We needed a GPS to help us find our way around in an unfamiliar and very populated area. We had a GPS, but in our packing, we misplaced the cord that plugged it into our car. We searched everywhere to no avail. We were staying at the home of friends the night before we left, and our friend tried every cord he could find to see if it would work on our GPS, but nothing worked. In the morning, we were about ready to say goodbye and step out the door to leave, when another friend of ours came to say goodbye and to give us a gift. "We thought you would need this," she said. It was a new GPS, exactly like the one we had, with cord and all. We shared with her the story of what had happened, which she had known nothing about. As believers in God, we all marveled at how he sometimes orchestrates such goodness to show us he is with us and loves us. God's providence is working in all of our lives to make good things happen, whether they are seemingly insignificant things or life-saving things; whether they are personal for my benefit or enabling his work to be accomplished through me for the benefit of others.

In the following few paragraphs, I will elaborate on the fact that the God of the Bible, whom I consider worthy of my worship, is the one who does things like this. Others may worship a different kind of power, whether they call it God or something else. For example, it could be they believe in the power of nature or fate or the stars in their horoscope or a pantheistic god or the god of some other religion. When these kinds of things happen in their lives, they will likely attribute these events to their god or gods or whatever they deem worthy of their worship. Others would say that these coincidental or chance kinds of events could happen at any time, and it doesn't mean any so-called god was the cause. True enough, but when you trust your god, it is reasonable to attribute these mysterious workings to that which you worship.

I worship the God I have found to be true according to his Word, the Bible. His Word tells me he loves and cares about me, and when providential things like I just shared happen in my life, it is easy to attribute them to the God who shows up to let me know he really does care about me. If there is a God as portrayed in the Bible, as many people with good reason strongly believe, then when he tells us what he is like and what he will do, it makes sense that we would recognize him as the cause of those good and wondrous, unexpected, amazing, and astonishing things that happen.

Consider the following examples of God's providence from a few historical stories in the Old Testament of the Bible. A servant of Abraham was sent to look for a wife for Abraham's son. The servant asked God for help and experienced God's providential love in finding the right girl (Genesis 24). Here is how it happened. He traveled a long way to an unfamiliar country, and when he arrived, he rested at a well of water outside the city. He began talking to God and asking him to grant kindness to Abraham by sending a girl to the well who was the one Abraham's son was to marry. He said that he would recognize her as the one if he asked her for a drink, and she would volunteer to water his camels. Before he finished speaking, a woman came. He ran over to her and asked her for a drink. She volunteered to water his camels. When he further talked with her, he found out she was a daughter of Abraham's relatives, and as it turned out, she was the one who went back with him to marry Abraham's son. A lucky chance event or God's providential working?

In the opening of this chapter, I mentioned the story of Joseph. His story is a good example of how many bad things can happen to us, and yet God is working in the midst of those things to help us. When Joseph eventually met his brothers who had sold him into slavery, he assured them, "You meant it for evil, but God used it for good" (see his life's story in Genesis 37–50). When we go through troublesome times, we may think that God is not helping us. He seems to be absent, but if we keep trusting that he is with us, we can look back and see that he did work things out for good. To those who love God, he works all things together for good (Romans 8:28). We know too that God is good to those who do not believe. God wants them to repent of rejecting him, and he uses acts of kindness in their lives to bring them to faith in him. The Bible says that God's acts of kindness lead to repentance (Romans 2:4). Perhaps he wants to use you and me to perform those acts of kindness.

In the biblical book of Esther, the name of God is never mentioned, but you can definitely see God's hand in how things worked out for good in her life and in the lives of her people. One of the things that happened involved the planned death of Mordecai, a relative who raised Esther as his daughter. Haman, a man who hated Mordecai, planned to hang him the next day. The next day he went to the king to tell him his plan. But the king could not sleep the night before. He asked that a history book be brought to him, and in it was recorded how Mordecai had once saved his life. When Haman showed up in the morning with his plan to kill Mordecai, the king asked him how he would honor a person who the king wanted to honor. Haman, thinking that it was him the king wanted to honor, told him what he should do to honor that person. What a shock and reversal of his plan when the king told him to go and honor Mordecai that way. So Haman was now parading through the city, honoring the man he planned to kill. Clearly, it was as if something, or someone, ordered many such events in the story of Esther. Were those events fate, chance happenstance, or God?

A question arises concerning providential happenings. If you experience a providential event, does this mean that any god you believe in, whatever or whomever it may be, is the cause of the event? In other words, if you believe in the power of witchcraft, horoscopes, or the God of the Bible, is that object of your trust what causes such happenings in your life? Or is there only one God who causes them? As I said above, providential happenings do not prove the existence of a God; however, most people believe in some superhuman power greater than themselves because, in truth, we humans are needy and cannot control everything as we would like.

The world around us can be cruel, and we find ourselves unable, without help, to deal with the problems and fears we face. According to the Bible, there is no other God but the God and Father of Christ Jesus (Isaiah 45:5; Matthew 3:16-17). Therefore, if you worship some other power, you would be worshiping what is false or unable to deliver all that you would hope for. This is not to say there are no other supernatural powers in the world—there are satanic powers trying to persuade us of other gods—but the God of the Bible is the only one who can give a person the greatest of blessings, working to do a person good and meet a need, and giving to that person a most satisfying life, one that never ends.

If there is only one God, the God of the Bible, how can we know such to be true and that our object of worship needs to be that particular God, and thus that he is the one responsible for the providential acts that I experience? One of the ways the God of the Bible demonstrates his power to be superior to all other objects of people's trust and worship is by the miraculous works he performs in history. His miracles cannot be outdone by any other source of power, and although some superhuman powers can be displayed by other sources, none can match certain miracles by God. For example, when Moses and his brother, Aaron, were in Egypt, trying to convince Pharaoh to give the Hebrew slaves their freedom, Pharaoh wanted to know what God could be more powerful than his gods. Aaron threw his wooden staff on the floor, and it turned into a snake. To Pharaoh, this was no big deal, for his religious people came and did the same thing by throwing down their staffs. However, God's snake ate up their snakes (Exodus 7:8-12).

Another powerful thing God did, which became known among the surrounding nations and people of that time, was to save his people from Egypt's army. He did this by parting the Red Sea, allowing his people to get away and Pharaoh's army chasing after them to perish (Exodus 14:9-31; Joshua 2:8-11). I am aware that many persons call such biblical events myths and not true history, but one reason I believe in the accurate history of the Bible is the trustworthiness of the Bible's New Testament documents. Being skeptical and having investigated many facts concerning those documents, I've found them reliable and believable. That being the case, the written reports about Jesus' words and works, with good reason, can be taken to be true. If Jesus believes the Old Testament documents and events to be historically true, so do I (for example, see Matthew 12:38-41). Therefore, if through trustworthy records Jesus says there is a God, and he believes in the miracles of God that were recorded in the Old Testament, I believe him. It is thus quite reasonable for me to believe that my providential experiences are the effects of the God and Father of Jesus Christ.

What about God's providential love and works toward people who consider themselves bad people? We have mentioned that Romans 2:4 says God's kindness leads to repentance. Jesus said God does good to all people (Matthew 5:45). Yes, bad people experience God's goodness too. Consider that God may show his goodness through bad things that happen to them, to awaken their conscience with thoughts like, *What's happening in my life is not good and not right*, or, *I wish I wasn't this way.* Such thoughts may be God trying to get that person's attention by saying, *You need to seek me and let me change you.* The providence of God may also bring other people into a bad person's life to speak through that person to try and help them—maybe someone who cares for them. God may also work providentially to help a person see the need to change by allowing that person to get caught or in trouble for their crimes or bad behaviors. Even though there is an evil power in the world trying to destroy people's lives by telling them to continue in their ways or reinforcing their thoughts that they are clever and smart and will not get caught, God loves all people and does not want them to perish (Ezekiel 18:23, 32; 2 Peter 3:9). However, if persons continue to reject God's attempts to get their attention, at some point he will have no choice but to let them go their own self-chosen and self-destructive way and reap the results (Proverbs 29:1; Romans 1:18-25).

Is it God's providence when bad things happen to good people? Not all things that happen to us are of God's doing. Yes, God could prevent bad things from happening (Daniel 3:24-27), and some disastrous events may be his judgments against evil (Numbers 21:6). But we, by our own will and choices, are responsible for many of the bad things that happen to us. For example, my health can be affected by eating wrong or failing to exercise as I ought. Accidents are often the result of an unawareness of dangers or not being careful to prevent them. Sin in people is another cause of bad things that happen to us. How much suffering in the world is caused by powerlessness over destructive addictive behaviors? We are victims from many kinds of wrongs by others that cause our pain or suffering. Also, because sin and evil have come into this world, bad things happen as a natural part of the world we live in. For example, we have no control over storms or diseases that happen because of the nature of a corrupted earth that is awaiting its redemption (Romans 8:20-22). However, even though we may not attribute every bad thing that happens to us as God's doing, we do have the responsibility to respond to bad things as an opportunity to examine our ways and correct anything in us or around us that may need correcting (Luke 13:1-5).

141

Should believers accept bad things that happen to them as God's way of disciplining them to make them better persons? The Bible does say that God disciplines us for our good that we might share his holiness (Hebrews 12:5-11). Yes, he may allow and use evil happenings to discipline us, and we can learn and grow stronger in our faith from evil things that happen to us, but I do not think that is the primary means of God's discipline. Rather, a primary way God disciplines us is through the words of Scripture that are meant to correct us and set us on the right path (2 Timothy 3:16-17). He speaks those words by his Holy Spirit who indwells us as his children, and unless I am in a rebellious state, I find that his words are spoken not angrily but with patience and gentleness. But because we all differ, God knows the best way to reach our hearts.

Another way he disciplines us is through the rebukes and punishments of people he puts as authorities in our lives, particularly parents, teachers, bosses at work, police, and government officials. He may use friends or family members who tell us honestly, although it may hurt us, that we need to change something that is not good about ourselves. If we want to avoid God's discipline, one of the best ways is to take responsibility to discipline ourselves (1 Timothy 4:7-8) and to make wrong things right within us and in our situations with others.

God is not the author or cause of evil, which would make him less than good, but sometimes he may allow us to experience the consequences of evil in our lives to awaken us from being comfortable with any evil in us, sometimes without our being aware of it. I have an idea that in a world like ours, where evil is so ingrained in and around us, we may need to experience its destructiveness so we can see what it is doing to us. It is therefore good for God to allow it if it brings us to the place of hating evil and needing to trust and rely on God to help us change. Sometimes he uses evildoers to come against people as a judgment and punishment for their sins, especially if they are so far astray from him that repentance can occur in no other way.

CLOSING REMINDERS

I want to come back from these few digressions to the original kind of God's providence that surprises us with good things in our lives to let us know he cares for us and loves us. We all suffer from evils and hardships in this world, and he wants us to find strength and peace by casting our fears and anxieties on him, remembering that he cares for us (1 Peter 5:6-11). God is for us and with us, and he will fight for us to help us defeat all evil. I made a list of God's providential events in my life so that if or when I doubt that God is for me and with me, I can recall those times he did wonderful things for me to let me know he has me in mind and has not abandoned me. Following are four things I want to reiterate in closing, things we need to remember in times of doubt and stress, things that will give us renewed courage and perseverance.

First, God is doing something good in our lives, even when bad things seem to prevail over us. Most often we do not see what God is doing until later, even much later. Joseph had much bad happen in his life, yet he could say, "You meant evil against me, but God meant it for good . . . to preserve many people alive" (Genesis 50:20-25). We must trust God and make sure we desire his good will in our lives and not wrong or evil things. God will judge all evil and wickedness that comes against us and destroy it; but not yet, for in his perfect wisdom, he knows the valuable purpose evil can serve in an evil world. And let us not forget that God causes all things to work together for good to those who love him. We become stronger against evil, our faith grows, and we become more like Christ Jesus in our character (Romans 5:3-5; 8:28-29; James 1:2-4).

Second, God loves us and the world he created and is with us whether or not we can see it. You and I may be going through some afflictions caused by evil, like Habakkuk when he complained to God about why he was using the wicked to surround and swallow up the righteous (Habakkuk 1:2-4, 13). But God's answer to him is that he will use it for good, and we must trust him. Habakkuk believes God and says this, which we can also say: "I will exult in the Lord, I will rejoice in the God of my salvation. The Lord is my strength . . . and makes me walk on my high places" (Habakkuk 3:16-19). If bad things are happening to us like they were to Job, we need to respond like him: "Though he slay me, I will hope in him" (Job 13:15). We need to not be afraid but believe that God will take care of us. "Greater is he who is in you than he who is in the world" (1 John 4:4).

Third, one thing we can conclude from this chapter is this: God is good to all people (Psalm 145:8-9), and through his providential acts, he is showing that he loves and cares about us. I may not understand why God chooses not to intervene in the world and keep evil from happening, but he does promise that a perfect and evil-free world is in his future plans for me. Even if I suffer bad things, I must persevere in hope and faith as I await the prize God has for me (Revelation 2:26-27). God will not allow evil to defeat us. He will fight for us, and he invites us to join him in the battle. I can say with Esther, "If I perish, I perish," knowing that even in death, we will live again (1 Corinthians 6:14).

Finally, to end where we began in this chapter, I must share another story to reiterate that *God is with us.* One late night, alone in the car, I was driving home down a two-lane road on which there were no other cars. Wanting to get through a green light before it turned red, I sped up a little. As I neared the green light, I heard a voice in my head that said one urgent sounding word, *STOP.* For some reason, I obeyed the voice and put on the brake. It slowed me down enough that a car, having run the red light, flashed across directly in front of me and just missed hitting me broadside. My heart was racing the rest of the way home. I never saw the car approaching that intersection, and all I could conclude was that God was responsible for giving me a warning that saved me from harm and possible death. Perhaps you will be encouraged to recall and share with others your stories of God's goodness. Your family, grandkids, friends, acquaintances, or even strangers, may be greatly blessed and strengthened in their faith. When we have a need or are going through rough times, the promise that God is with us is a promise we want never to forget.

CHAPTER 9

LOVE AND MONEY

I include a chapter on this subject of love and money because there are two key passages in the Bible that connect love with money—one negative and the other positive. The negative connection of love with money is found in 1 Timothy 6:10. It reads, "For the love of money is the root of all sorts of evil, and some by longing for it have wandered away from the faith and pierced themselves with many griefs." As leaders in the church, Timothy and other church leaders must be free from the love of money (1 Timothy 3:1-3). Because we all deal with money, it is a relevant warning for all of us. The positive side of love and money is conveyed in 1 Timothy 6:17-19 where the rich are told to "fix their hope on God, who richly supplies us with all things to enjoy." Love for God motivates us to use our money "to do good, to be rich in good works, to be generous and ready to share."

God warns us against the *love* of money, not against money itself. Being wealthy is not a problem with God. Abraham, the father of our Christian faith (Galatians 3:6-9), was a wealthy man (Genesis 13:2; 24:34-35). Job, who God calls a righteous man, was very wealthy (Job 1:1-3; 42:12). Joseph of Arimathea, a good and righteousness man, a man who did not agree with the Jewish Council's vote to put Jesus to death, was granted permission from the Roman governor to bury Jesus' body in his tomb (Luke 23:50-53). Scripture noted that he was a rich man (Matthew 27:57). Obviously, God does not bless all of us with great wealth; nevertheless, money is needed by all of us for the support of self, family, and daily living. Whether we have little or much, all of us need to be aware of both the negatives and the positives when it comes to love and money. A good place to begin our study is to hear what Jesus has to say about money. His, and other biblical teachings, will guide us toward right attitudes about money as well as how to use the money God gives us in a way that honors him.

THE NEGATIVE ABOUT MONEY: LOVE OF MONEY

The following teachings will help us understand what is meant by the *love of money*. In Luke 12:13-15, a man spoke out from a crowd of people and said to Jesus, "Tell my brother to divide the family inheritance with me." Evidently, there was a bit of a family feud going on over an inheritance, and this man wanted his share. Jesus responded with a warning that everyone gathered in that crowd could hear. He said, "Beware, and be on your guard against every form of greed; for not even when one has an abundance does his life consist of his possessions." A primary meaning of *greed* involves an attitude and practice of coveting. One of God's Ten Commandments is, "Do not covet" (Exodus 20:17). Greed and coveting are impelling desires to have more. It is a passionate longing, a lusting after, an inner drive to want money and whatever money can buy. Although it is not wrong to want what we need, and although God is not opposed to being wealthy, the negative side is making our desire for money or possessions something that consumes our life. As in 1 Timothy 6:10, quoted above, "By longing for it, many wander away from the faith." Money takes priority over God.

Notice, in Luke 12:15, that Jesus said two things about greed and coveting. First, he said, "Guard yourself against every form of greed." We can't guard ourselves against greed if we don't recognize it. How do we know if we are covetous? We can know by recognizing the many forms it may take in our lives (Romans 7:7-8). One form of greed is an inner and overwhelming desire to want more, and to get what we want, we can easily fall into wrong actions such as cheating or stealing. I remember as a kid, I wanted a baseball glove. I had some money I had earned mowing lawns, but I wanted the glove right away, and I did not have enough money. I knew where my parents kept a jar of coins. I stole some and bought the glove. It's easy to do wrong when we have an overwhelming desire or need to want more than we have.

Another form of recognizable greed is planning and scheming to take advantage of others for the sake of one's own gain. I know of doctors who leave their place of employment because they are pressured or forced by their employers to spend less time caring for patients so they can see more patients and make more money. The employers call helping more people good business sense, but the doctor who genuinely wants to help others get well suffers along with the patients when he knows they are getting less care.

Another show of greed is from those who take advantage of others by raising prices above what is reasonable or fair because there is increased demand for a product. Yet another form of greed is evident in people who develop life-dominating habits such as gambling or chasing quick-money-making schemes. Greed may also be present when people use smooth talk or false promises to trick or manipulate others into giving them something they want. Hoarding things for oneself, or to withhold giving help to persons in need even though you have the means, may be other ways we can detect greed. Jesus points out that there are many forms of greed and covetousness.

A second thing Jesus said about greed in Luke 12:15 is that "life does not consist of one's possessions." Much of our world is run by the desire for money as if money is what life is all about. Love of money corrupts people. The Bible makes a point of saying that in these last days, before Christ Jesus returns to earth, difficult times will come. Why? Because people will be lovers of self, lovers of money, unloving, and so forth, rather than lovers of God (2 Timothy 3:1-4). It seems that life, for much of today's world, has become all about living for material things and pleasures.

One of the lessons that the Covid-19 pandemic days has shown us is how quickly the material things we enjoy can be taken away. Sports events were gone, eating out at restaurants and visiting shopping malls was curtailed, businesses and schools were shut down, money investments were significantly decreased or lost, and even church buildings were closed for meetings. The Bible reminds us, "Do not weary yourself to gain wealth, cease from your consideration of it. When you set your eyes on it, it is gone. For wealth certainly makes itself wings like an eagle that flies toward the heavens" (Proverbs 23:4-5). Living through those pandemic days should teach us, as Jesus is trying to do, that life does not consist of one's possessions. Life consists of something greater than what is earthly and temporary.

Jesus taught more about money in Luke 16:13: "No servant can serve two masters; for either he will hate the one and love the other, or else he will be devoted to the one and despise the other. You cannot serve God and wealth." Some religious leaders who were lovers of money were scoffing at Jesus' words. They saw no problem with having money along with serving God. It is easy to justify what we do so that we feel what we are doing is all right. Jesus said to lovers of money that they may justify their actions in the sight of men, but God knows their hearts, and what they value in this world is detestable in the sight of God (Luke 16:14-15). In other words, these religious persons were entrusted with the job of serving others with God's words of truth and deeds of goodness, but they allowed their lust for money to interfere with faithfully administering God's love and life to people.

You and I might also be tempted to make light of Jesus' words. We may think, *Wait a minute, I thought God had no objections to being wealthy.* True, but remember, we are not talking about being wealthy, we are speaking of the love of money and how it corrupts people. The Bible stresses the point that greed is idolatry (Colossians 3:5). God is to be first in our lives, and when we worship something else, it takes us away from God. Why should God be first? Because he is the only source of real life, goodness, peace, and a love that makes us ultimately fulfilled and whole. To go away from him is foolish because it deprives us of what is good and lasting that God alone can give.

Remember what 1 Timothy 6:10 said: "Money is the root of all sorts of evil, and some by longing for it have wandered away from the faith and pierced themselves with many griefs." The verse before it says, "But those who want to get rich fall into temptation and a snare and many foolish and harmful desires which plunge men into ruin and destruction" (1 Timothy 6:9). A seemingly minor experience as a kid taught me the truth of this verse. I wanted to be richer, fell into temptation, and lost all I had. I was at our county fair where I saw all the great prizes I could win at the game booths. I wanted those prizes, and the person running one of those games lured me in by telling me how I could play and win. So I paid him some money and tried it but did not win. He told me that he would double my winnings if I would try again. Because I wanted those prizes, I kept listening to the man until I lost all of my money. A foolish and harmful desire plunged me into ruin. I told myself I would never do that again, and I didn't.

A huge indication that we are putting money and possessions ahead of God is the fear of losing what we have. When losing our money and possessions is threatened, fear reveals our dependence on money instead of our trust in God. Think about how much fear people who have money experience when their financial investments and savings drop by thousands of dollars or more during times of economic recession. If trust in God's ability to care for us is overlooked in favor of dependence on money, what does that say about what we are trusting to provide for our well-being? "You of little faith," Jesus said in Matthew 6:30. Jesus taught that we are to first seek God's kingdom and his righteousness and not to worry about ending up with nothing, for God cares and will take care of us (Matthew 6:25-34). Granted, this is easier said than done. Admittedly, trusting God is tough when things do not go in the direction we want. All I will say here is that God has good reason for whatever he does or does not do. We are tempted to dismiss God if we think prayer and faith in him are not working. Trials grow our faith, and hanging on to him and his promises gives us hope that positive results will come. Jesus did not enjoy being mocked, beaten, and nailed to a cross, but he kept his faith in God and accepted God's will, and the results were astounding.

Freedom from the Love of Money

Hebrews 13:5-6 says, "Make sure that your character is free from the love of money, being content with what you have; for He Himself has said, 'I will never desert you, nor will I ever forsake you,' so that we may confidently say, 'The Lord is my helper, I will not be afraid. What will man do to me?'"

One of the things freeing us from the love of money is contentment. Contentment, no matter what our circumstances, makes us free. The Apostle Paul's life was up and down. Sometimes he had little; sometimes he had much. Sometimes he received good results in ministering to people; sometimes all he received was beatings. Sometimes people believed his message; sometimes people laughed and would not believe. Sometimes he was fearful of his surroundings; sometimes he was brave and confident. Sometimes he felt alone; sometimes he felt people supported him. Sometimes he felt a failure; sometimes he felt successful. Sometimes he went hungry; sometimes he had food. Sometimes he had abundance; sometimes he suffered need. In spite of ups and downs, he says, "I have learned to be content in whatever circumstances I am" (Philippians 4:11-12).

What does contentment mean and how do we learn it? Contentment means not desiring something more or different but being satisfied with whatever. Contentment means I have something sufficient within myself so that changes in my life, good or bad, don't affect who I am. This inner sufficiency can be in oneself or in something or someone else. Contentment to some comes by self-sufficiency where people say to themselves that they can do without. They suppress their desires or wants and choose to get through a tough time by their own strength of will. There is some truth in this for all of us, but for believers in God, contentment is a kind of sufficiency that doesn't need or want anything, not because of suppressing one's desires and relying on oneself but because of learning to rely on God to take care of them in their situation. For example, the Apostle Paul says his contentment is because "I can do all things through Christ who strengthen me" (Philippians 4:13). The writer of Hebrews 13:5-6 can be free from the love of money and be content with what he has because he knows God is always present with him and will help him. His contentment comes from sensing the presence of God in his life and not being afraid. True contentment is what is conveyed in Psalm 23: "The Lord is my shepherd, I shall not want." We have all we want because we receive all we want from the Lord.

This thought is conveyed in another psalm, which says, "Whom have I in heaven *but You*? And besides You, I desire nothing on earth" (Psalm 73:25). Contentment does not come by acquiring wealth or material things that satisfy us and make us feel secure. Contentment comes by building a relationship with God the Father and the Son. We are complete in him and his promises, not in ourselves or in what we have. Building our relationship with him, having godly character and trust in him, is what enables contentment. This point is made in 1 Timothy 6:6-8 where we are told that "godliness is a means of great gain when accompanied by contentment." Contentment comes out of godliness, which is relying on God and becoming like God in our character. Contentment knows that nothing in this world matters since all is temporary and passes away, but what matters are the eternal things we find in God that can never be lost.

Someone said that contentment is freedom from wanting things but not freedom from needing things. There is a sense in which this is true. We still need things to be able to live, and even though we may be content with our needy and less than desirable circumstances, to take responsibility for our well-being does not imply discontentment. We are often expected by God to do the proper things to get our needs met. For example, the Apostle Paul can be hungry and without the food he needs. Although content in that circumstance, he can choose to do something about it. He can ask for help, as he did with the people of the Philippian church (Philippians 4:10-14), or he can find work to support himself (2 Thessalonians 3:8). In other words, being content does not mean fatalism, accepting one's fate as though it is set in concrete. God created us as agents of change, and if we have opportunity, we can do something about meeting our needs so as not to be a burden to others. Paul said, "If anyone is not willing to work," let him not eat (2 Thessalonians 3:10).

Another example of contentment in daily life is seen when John the Baptist preached for people to repent of their sins and live their life in a godly way. Some soldiers ask John, "What shall we do?" John told them, "Do not take money from anyone by force, or accuse anyone falsely, and be content with your wages" (Luke 3:14). If one of those soldiers did not have enough to provide for his family's needs, there is nothing to prevent him from asking for an increase in wages; but still, no matter what, his life needed to be characterized by contentment and not by the love of money.

How can a person be content when his or her needs are not being met? Rather than simply suppressing our passions and desires, we let our feelings and requests be made known to God (Philippians 4:6-7). Instead of suppressing our passions and desires, we learn to trust God and rely on him to meet our needs and even to give us the desires of our hearts, expressing thanks to him in whatever his answer might be, whether it's soon, later, or not at all. In other words, we become free from want because we believe God loves us, is present with us, and will not abandon us. Jesus is our supreme example. When going through his horrible sufferings and death, what gave him peace and contentment was his knowledge and faith in God the Father's presence and promises (Acts 2:24-28). Consider also Luke 12:22-32 where Jesus tells us not to worry about our needs and why. We experience contentment when we are convinced of the Lord's presence and care (1 Peter 5:7).

LOVE AND THE POSITIVE USE OF MONEY

At the beginning of this chapter, I stated that there are two key passages in the Bible that connect love with money—one negative and the other positive. We shall now consider the positive connection between love and money. Instead of the love of money guiding its negative use, the love of God guides its positive use. In 1 Timothy 6:11 people who belong to God are encouraged to pursue godly character, which includes righteousness and love. This God-like love provides the motivation and reason behind people's positive use of their money.

Here is a side thought. First Timothy 6:11 is obviously given in the context of money riches, but people can be rich in other ways. They can be rich in love, in relationships, in the hope of eternal things promised by God, in peace, and so forth. Whether financially rich or poor, the instruction is the same for both: a person's love for God and the value he puts on people determines the use of one's money. This means even the poor, although not able to do as much good with the little bit of money they have, can still do much good with the riches they have other than money. It doesn't take much money to help others going through tough times with needed love or friendship or words of encouragement and hope. Whatever we have that is given to us by God is not to be hoarded and kept only for self but is to be used for the good of others.

With that in mind, let's consider the instruction that those rich in money are to practice (1 Timothy 6:17-19). First, do not be *conceited* (1 Timothy 6:17). This word means don't be arrogant, proud, high-minded, and self-absorbed. Jesus told a story about a farmer who tore down his barns to build bigger ones. He had so much success at his business that his wealth kept growing and he needed more places to put it all (Luke 12:15-21). He thought his future was secure because of the wealth he had. He said to himself, "'Soul, you have many goods laid up for many years; take your ease, eat, drink, and be merry.' But God called him a fool, saying, 'This very night your soul is required of you, and who will own what you have prepared?'" (Luke 12:19-20). Why is he called a fool? Certainly, he is not a fool because he was a hard worker and had accumulated much wealth, for that is an admirable trait. Jesus said he was a fool because he failed to consider the truth about the next life, and in thinking only of himself, he was not rich toward God. To think riches in this life was all he needed to give him satisfaction and security would be a bit presumptuous, even arrogant. If he knew there was a God, he should have thought there was more to life than what he was experiencing. He thought only of himself, having no thought of God, the future God has planned, nor of God's interest in him having loving concern for others. He was mistaken to think that life's security and meaning is found in the things of this world rather than in the eternal things of God.

As a kid, I started a collection of bird nests. One day, I felt a stabbing pain in my soul. I thought, *Why am I doing this? It won't last. One day it will all rot or be gone, I will die, and what difference will it have made?* I suddenly lost interest in doing it and quit. I can see now that there would not have been anything wrong with such a hobby, so long as I also understood that I needed to give my life to something that was lasting. In that moment, I realized there was something more to life than material things that are temporary. I wanted something eternal. Many years later, I discovered that I had experienced what Solomon wrote about in his biblical book of Ecclesiastes, that working only for the things this life can give you is vanity (Ecclesiastes 2:18-20; 3:9-11). We were made for more than what this world offers. One point of Jesus' story was this: don't be conceited in thinking that life revolves around you and what you want and what you can get for yourself.

Another way money can make us conceited, proud, or arrogant is to think that because we have money, we are better than or above or more popular than others. It is easy to use the power of money as a way to impress others and make oneself look good or feel important. This is how the prodigal son used his inherited money, and he ended with nothing until he came back to his Father, who, in the story, represented God (Luke 15:11-24).

I don't want us to miss the last part of 1 Timothy 6:17, which says God "richly supplies us with all things to enjoy." It has to please God to see us enjoying the world he has created for us. It's like a parent giving a gift to a child. They take great pleasure in seeing their child get excited to receive it and to see them enjoying it. After all, that is why they gave it. Similarly, as we enjoy this world, we ought to be thankful to God for all the things he has given us.

Here is another thought. The Bible asks us in 1 Corinthians 4:7, "What do you have that you did not receive? And if you did receive it, why do you boast as if you had not received it?" Nothing in life was gotten on our own without the help of others. Therefore, gladly and willingly, we ought to thank others for whatever they do for us, and with hearts full of thankfulness, it makes sense to share what we have with family, friends, neighbors, and those in need.

That being said, let's go to 1 Timothy 6:18, which tells us how God wants the rich to use the money entrusted to them. God instructs them "to do good, to be rich in good works, to be generous and ready to share." This is not just for the rich. The Bible says all Christ followers are to labor with their own hands what is good, so that they will have something to share with one who has need (Ephesians 4:28). "Laboring with your own hands what is good" means not being lazy and not using evil ways to earn your money.

What we do to help others in this world is doing what God the Father and Jesus the Son do. Actually, we are doing it on God's behalf. God tells us to love our neighbor. Like the Good Samaritan who spent his money to help a stranger, Jesus said for us to go and do the same (Luke 10:29-37). Jesus said that when we come across people who are hungry or in need of clothing or are sick or in prison, when we reach out to help them, we are doing it to him, for those are people Jesus cares about (Matthew 25:34-40). Proverbs 19:17 says, "The one who is gracious to the poor lends to the Lord, and he will repay him for his good deed."

Jesus said, "For you always have the poor with you, and whenever you wish you can do good to them" (Mark 14:7). The poor are on God's heart. They need help. Who are the poor? I searched the internet for articles on the subject. Many studies say much of what we may already know. The poor are those with the lowest standards of living in a society. They barely have enough money to maintain their current conditions, and they lack the educational opportunities and resources to better their lives. Some are without necessities like clean drinking water, food, or adequate housing. They may see themselves as trapped with no control over their situation, having to be content with whatever they can get to survive. I am thinking that the best way to decide whom to help is not to classify people as poor but to discover people's needs. Those with adequate resources are to help any persons God brings across their path, not based on judging a person's social status, ethnic group, or worthiness, but based on need.

This brings me to the final thing 1 Timothy says about love and money. By our godly use of money, God promises that we are storing up for ourselves the treasure of a good foundation for the future (1 Timothy 6:19). Jesus said the same thing, that in using money for

God's purposes, rather than storing up treasures on earth, we are storing up treasures in heaven (Matthew 6:19-21).

Returning to 1 Timothy 6:17, the Bible instructs those with money to "not fix your hope on the uncertainty of riches, but on God, who richly supplies us with all things to enjoy." We have already noted the biblical truth that wealth can quickly be gone (Proverbs 23:4-5). According to our present text, we are to fix our hope on God. Hope means to believe in something future, things that are certain to happen, things you look forward to that are good, especially things that God promises.

I remember times my grandfather took me with him to work. He was groundskeeper for a rich family with a large estate and big mansion. We would enter through a tall iron gate, and I would play in the outdoor swimming pool while he worked. Sometimes, when riding in a car down roads with large, enclosed estates like that, seeing them would make me feel envious, and I would think how great it would be to have that for my home. The thought didn't last long, for then I remembered the Bible's promise that God is preparing a place for me. That is my hope, and knowing it to be true, I thought, *I don't need such a house now, I can wait. One day God will provide a much grander place for me to live* (John 14:1-3).

Moses grew up in a king's palace. He could have had all the riches and passing pleasures of sin that Egypt had to offer, but he refused it all and chose to endure ill-treatment with God's people. He considered identification with Christ greater riches than the treasures of Egypt, for he was looking to the reward (Hebrews 11:24-26). He put his hope in the rewarding promises of Christ. The same is true with Abraham. He lived in tents in a place he considered temporary until he received his promised inheritance from God. He believed in the things God promised him, and even though he died without receiving them, he looked forward to a better country, a heavenly one, with a city whose builder and maker was God (Hebrews 11:8-16).

One day, surrounded by the beauty of Montana where my wife and I lived for most of our lives, I suddenly became very saddened. I did not want to leave this earth. I had become attached to the big sky's clear lakes and streams, the prairies and mountains, the breathtaking sunsets and starry skies. The sadness left me when I realized that I will not have to leave God's beautiful earth because he plans to restore all things. Faithful believers in Christ Jesus will inherit the world with its new earth (Acts 3:19-21; Romans 4:13; 8:18-25; 2 Peter 3:13). Although we enjoy this present world and the riches it offers, we do not fix our hope on the uncertainty of riches in this life but on God who will again, in his future world, richly supply us with all things to enjoy (1 Timothy 6:17). *The love of money* will destroy a person's life. But *the love of God*, with godliness, kindness, and love in using money for his good purposes, will result in our grand entrance into the coming kingdom of God (2 Peter 1:10-11).

I leave you with a few wise sayings to ponder about money from biblical proverbs. They are all true in their proper life contexts:

"Honor the LORD from your wealth and from the first of all your produce; so your barns will be filled with plenty and your vats will overflow with new wine" (3:9-10).

"Riches do not profit in the day of wrath, but righteousness delivers from death" (11:4).

"He who trusts in his riches will fall, but the righteous will flourish like the green leaf" (11:28).

"Wealth obtained by fraud dwindles, but the one who gathers by labor increases it" (13:11).

"Better is a little with the fear of the Lord than great treasure and turmoil with it" (15:16).

"He who gives to the poor will never want, but he who shuts his eyes will have many curses" (28:27).

"The acquisition of treasures by a lying tongue is a fleeting vapor, the pursuit of death" (21:6).

"The rich and poor have a common bond, the Lord is the maker of them all" (22:2).

"The reward of humility and the fear of the Lord are riches, honor, and life" (22:4).

"Do not weary yourself to gain wealth, cease from your consideration of it. When you set your eyes on it, it is gone. For wealth certainly makes itself wings like an eagle that flies toward the heavens" (23:4-5).

"Better is the poor who walks in his integrity than he who is crooked though he be rich" (28:6).

"A faithful man will abound with blessings, but he who makes haste to be rich will not go unpunished" (28:20).

"Two things I asked of You, do not refuse me before I die: keep deception and lies far from me, give me neither poverty nor riches; feed me with the food that is my portion, that I not be full and deny You and say, 'Who is the LORD?' Or that I not be in want and steal, and profane the name of my God" (30:7-9).

Remember, God is not opposed to riches, only to wrong motives, wrong ways of gaining them, and their misuse.

CHAPTER 10

WHAT DOES IT MEAN TO LOVE GOD?

There was once a lawyer who was an expert in knowing the laws that God gave to Moses. He suspected that a new teacher on the scene was leading people astray. One thing he did not like was that Jesus claimed to be equal with God. He wanted to tell people not to listen to this teacher, but apparently, he needed proof to show people that his teachings were false. So, one day, wanting to test Jesus to see if he had the right teachings and was worth listening to, he asked Jesus a question: "Teacher, what is the great commandment of God's Law?" Jesus answered, "You shall love the Lord your God with all your heart, and with all your soul, and with all your mind. This is the great and foremost commandment" (Matthew 22:34-38). He was quoting the most important law that Moses was to teach the people of Israel (Deuteronomy 6:1-5). This law applies to all people who claim to believe in the biblical God, including present day persons who claim to follow Christ Jesus.

The title of this chapter has been a very important question for me to answer. I want to know what loving God means because of something Jesus said about religious people who called Jesus their Lord. Thinking they had lived as God wanted and were approved by him, and believing they will enter heaven, Jesus will say, "I never knew you, depart from me" (Matthew 7:21-23). Obviously, there must be more to a right relationship with God than what they thought. *Knowing* God implies being approved by God and experiencing a personal connection of acceptance by him. His acceptance comes by our faith in the meaning of Jesus's death on the cross, and God's declaration that we are forgiven and are at peace with him (Romans 5:1-2). I need to be sure I have the Lord's acceptance through faith in Christ Jesus, which I believe I have. But beyond that, apparently there is the possibility that I could shrink away from him in shame at his coming (1 John 2:28). When we meet the Lord Jesus in person, will we be able to throw our arms around one another in a warm and welcoming embrace? I don't want to get there and be one who shies away, feeling ashamed or embarrassed because something was lacking in our relationship. What does it mean to love God, why should I, and how do we do it?

Loving God begins by opening up our hearts to be loved by him. It is difficult to love anybody if we ourselves have not been loved by them. Many people have honestly shared with me that they cannot love their father, mother, or someone else, because they were abused and mistreated by those who should have loved them but were not able to do it. Because of such treatment, some even feel they are bad and do not deserve to be loved. It's hard to love someone who has not loved you. Why would it be different with God? Love begins by being loved. We cannot love God with a heart that doubts his love or feels undeserving or blames him for what goes wrong in our lives. We love God because he first loves us (1 John 4:19).

How do we know that he loves us? Many know about God, even believe in him, but they don't have a two-way loving relationship. They need a heart in sync with God's heart. What does God do to help them? God promises, "I will give you a new heart and put a new spirit within you" (Ezekiel 36:26). This is what Jesus meant when he said, "You must be born again" (John 3:7). Jeremiah the prophet

160

said that there is coming a day when people will no longer have to be taught to "'"know the Lord," for they will all know Me, from the least of them to the greatest of them,' declares the Lord, 'for I will forgive their iniquity and their sin I will remember no more'" (Jeremiah 31:34). Love begins with a change of heart, and that heart change happens when we experience his love, especially his forgiveness. We cannot love God when we think we are underserving. We cannot love God with a self-centered heart. We cannot love God with a cold heart that is angry and bitter. We cannot love God with a rebellious heart that refuses to be humble and accept what God says. That is why the psalm writer prayed, "Create in me a clean heart, O God" (Psalm 51:10). When we are loved and forgiven by him and receive a changed heart through the gift of His Holy Spirit (Romans 5:5), then we can learn and grow in our love for him.

Realizing the depth of God's love through his forgiveness greatly affects the depth of our love for him. Wanting to teach about the relationship between forgiveness and the ability to love, Jesus told a self-righteous man something about a sinful woman. He said, "Her sins, which are many, have been forgiven, for she loved much; but he who is forgiven little loves little" (Luke 7:47). Is Jesus saying that our ability to love God is related to the extent of our being loved and forgiven by God, and that if this man were forgiven more, he would love God more? Yes, and therefore, we ask ourselves, *Is God's forgiveness of me causing me to have, or want to have, a deeply-felt love for him?*

Suppose, after becoming a child of God and a follower of Jesus, you get angry with someone and say things you don't mean, and you treat them badly. Do you feel bad, and do you confess and believe you are forgiven (1 John 1:9)? That would be good. What if you do the same thing tomorrow . . . and the next day and the next day, and you keep hurting people you care about? Do you still believe you are forgiven? Consider doing what you may feel are worse sins. Suppose you give in to the temptation to get drunk on alcohol or do another drug to feel good or you abuse your child or engage in pornography. Do you feel bad, and do you confess and believe you are forgiven? What if you do the same thing tomorrow and the next day and the next day. Do you still believe you are forgiven, or do you start to wonder how God can keep forgiving you when you habitually do what displeases him? Do you start hating yourself or fearing God's punishment? Do you start feeling that God can't love someone like you? Do you feel like you can't change so you might as well give up trying to be good?

The truth is, God does keep loving and forgiving you. Do you believe this? You are still his beloved child, and he does not disown you. If you do keep believing that you are loved and forgiven in spite of your sinfulness, at some point it will dawn on you how great his love is, and it will humble you to not want to keep living the way you are. You will not be able to keep accepting his forgiveness and feel OK about a wrong you are doing. You know you must change, and you will begin asking in earnest for him to help you. When the greatness of his forgiving love sinks in (Psalms 103:10-12; Isaiah 43:25), his love motivates you to do all you can to become the person he created you to be (read Romans 6:1-14). As I said above, I say again: realizing the depth of God's love through his forgiveness will greatly affect the depth of our love for him.

We may not be perfect in our performance of love, but God looks at the motives of a person's heart (1 Samuel 16:7). He knows our desire, and he is pleased with our efforts to love him. A person who loves God is one who wants the same things God wants and who is willing to live life as God wants. Such a motivation is the same one Jesus had. Because he loved his Father, he lived by this rule of love: "Not my will, but your will be done" (Luke 22:42). Loving God involves feelings, but primarily, loving God is about doing his will (Matthew 12:50)—not from fear of God and laws demanding our obedience but from naturally and voluntarily loving him because he has first loved us. If the following seven actions of loving God are recognizably present in our lives, we can know that we love him. So what does it mean to love God?

PUT GOD ABOVE EVERYTHING

To love God means to put him above everything else in our lives (Exodus 20:1-4). God's people learned from his Ten Commandments that there is to be no other God before him—no idols. God is to have first place in our hearts, minds, and decisions. The Bible says that when we put something ahead of God, we are committing adultery (Ezekiel 16:35-39; James 4:4). Adultery means instead of being loyal and faithful to someone, we leave them for someone else. God hates to see his people leave him and go after other gods and lesser things. God says he is a jealous God (Exodus 20:5). He wants to keep us for himself. Is he an egotistical God to demand putting him first? No! God commands us to love him above all else and with our whole being, and to be faithful to him because he knows there is no one else who can do for us the things that he can do. He knows that our lives will be ruined if we have any other god or gods. He guards us for himself because he wants to give us the best life we could ever have (John 10:7-10; Romans 8:32). Therefore, we guard ourselves from idols and keep ourselves in his love (1 John 5:21; Jude 1:21).

Someone once asked me what my idol was—money, lustful pleasures, a drug, my family . . . what? I think I do put God first in my life, but upon further thought about this I had to answer, "Myself, I am the idol." I am my own idol when I am selfish or I fear others not accepting me, so I do not put what God wants ahead of what I want. Jesus once reprimanded some religious leaders for loving "the approval of men rather than the approval of God" (John 12:42-43). Peter did not put God first when he put man's interests ahead of God's (Mark 8:31-33). I pray that I recognize and guard myself against this kind of idolatry.

Worship Him

To love God means to worship him (Luke 4:8). What does it mean to worship? To worship anything or anyone that we call our god is to treat that god with respectful reverence and adoration. Realizing weaknesses and dangers that are in the world, most people worship something beyond themselves, believing that what they worship is good, wise, trustworthy, and powerful enough to meet their needs— for example, security, peace, blessings, protection, good health, and so forth. People worship by giving to their god their humble submission, prayers, and service, and living their god's prescribed lifestyle. For what their god does for them, they respond with praise and thanksgiving. Oftentimes, rituals are involved in worship.

There are all kinds of gods in the world, and they widely differ from each other. It would be foolish to worship something we do not know much about. It would be smart to consider if what or who we worship is truly worthy of our worship. Jesus believed there was only one God worthy of worship. One day he met a woman, and he spoke to her about this God. He told her that God is spirit, and those who worship him must worship in truth and spirit. He told her this God is the God of the Jews (John 4:19-26). What qualities and characteristics must our God or gods have to be worthy of our worship? That is the question each of us must answer. We can find the answer for the God Jesus recommends if we study to learn about the God of the Bible. He is the Father of Jesus.

Jesus taught believers to address God like this: "Our Father who is in heaven, hallowed be your name" (Matthew 6:9). What does it mean to hallow God's name? To hallow God's name means to worship him by honoring him as holy and sacred, attributing to him the supreme meaning of all that is good. There is nothing in God that is evil and sinful, and we are to stand in awe of him (Isaiah 29:23). We profane his name when we dishonor him by not being holy as he is holy, by disobeying what he says to do (Jeremiah 34:12-17; Exodus 20:18-20; Leviticus 10:1-3; Acts 5:1-11; Hebrews 10:30-31). God's holiness should create fear in people. Fear, however, is of two kinds.

Those who reject God will have cause to fear him in the sense of being terrified by his wrath, judgment, and punishment. Such fear is based on God's righteous laws which must be obeyed to gain God's acceptance. God's laws exist so we can know right from wrong, and knowing we are wrong will cause fear of punishment. For many, he is a God to be avoided for fear he will punish them for doing wrong (Genesis 3:8-11). All people should be afraid because, at some point, none can keep from breaking his laws. This fear is not a bad thing if it motivates us to become humble, repent of our wrongs, and come to Christ Jesus for his forgiveness. God loves us and wants us to repent and live (Ezekiel 18:32). Those who do come to Jesus, trusting him to be their savior from God's wrath, will no longer fear God's wrath and judgment.

Some people prefer to see God as mean, and they will not accept a God who demands, punishes, and restricts their freedom. They rebel, preferring to live life their own way. But real life cannot work that way. Consider, for example, what it would be like if people rebel against those in their lives who they consider as mean for restricting their freedoms, perhaps their boss, their government, their spouse, their teacher, or their parents. Life is likely not to go well for them. If the person you rebel against really is evil, rebellion is understandable, but not if, like God, the authority figure is good and cares about you. How you see the other person determines the kind of fear you have.

FEAR HIM

To love God means to fear God in a good sense (Proverbs 1:7; 9:10)—not a fear of punishment but of awe, reverence, respect, and thanksgiving. God does not punish believers; he disciplines and corrects them (Hebrews 12:5-11). To have a proper fear and love for God we need to make a clear distinction between his *judgement and punishment* and his *discipline and correction*. God lovingly and patiently corrects believers' wrongs, and though sometimes painful, they know it is for their good so that they can become the kind of person God has created them to be. Perfect love casts out any fear that involves punishment (1 John 4:18). Punishment creates the kind of fear that if we do something wrong, we will have something bad happen to us, and we will be made to suffer for the wrongs we have done. God does not punish true believers for their wrongs because Jesus has already suffered their punishment for them. "Hallowed be his name" means to love, give reverence to, and respect him in such a way that you actually want to please him and honor him by doing his will.

OBEY HIM

To love God means to obey his commandments (1 John 2:3-6). One of the first commandments we are to yield to is the command to be baptized (Matthew 28:19). Baptism was a common practice to the first century Jews and others—they knew what it meant.

Not understanding its meaning seems to make people today more hesitant to do it. Baptism, according to Romans 6:3-11, means that you have become united with Jesus in his death and resurrection. Many church groups practice baptism by immersion under water. The symbolism of this is that when you go under the water, you are dying to your old nature of letting wrong ways to live ruin your life. Coming up out of the water is being resurrected with Jesus, meaning you are a newly created person. You now want to live Christ's way, obeying his Word and not obeying your rebellious and destructive desires. When you believed in him, he gave you his Holy Spirit to help you (Acts 2:38-39). Baptism is a witness to the fact that you have become a believer and follower of Jesus. How you live thereafter is your continuing witness.

There are always tests in life to see if we are truly committed to obeying God's Word. Here is an example—a testing of my obedience or lack thereof. One day, I became convicted of a sin I had committed a long time ago. I cheated on a test when I was a student in school. The Holy Spirit's conviction did not leave me, and I knew God wanted me to write a letter to the teacher, confessing what I did and asking forgiveness. I kept putting off obeying him. I did not want to do it. I did not think I had to do it since it was a minor thing that happened long ago. I felt I had a good relationship with God, and I didn't feel I was suffering any bad things in my life because of it. But I discovered that whenever I wanted to be close to God, he would softly and gently remind me of the letter.

Finally, after five years, I wrote the letter. I didn't hear anything back, and I didn't need to hear anything back. God didn't kick me out of his family, nor did he reprimand me and say I was a bad person. I did not feel afraid of God; I still had a relationship with him, just not as close a one as I wanted. I did not fear punishment or something bad happening in my life, but I needed to overcome my selfish pride and do what God said because it was keeping me from having a close and loving relationship with him. It was a personal thing between God and me, and I think he wanted me to do it as a test to see if I loved him enough to do what he said. I felt a great relief when I did it, and my relationship with God was close again. Since then, whenever I sin against someone, I want to make amends with them as soon as possible. Obeying God preserves my loving relationship with him and with others. His ways are good and right, and they give us peace.

When a person becomes a believer and has become a child of God, God is a loving Father who teaches and corrects them so they can be good like God wants them to be (Hebrews 12:9-11). They give reverence to him and respect his love and wisdom and willingly receive his correction, knowing it is good for them. Christians do not live under God's laws in a legalistic sense (i.e., *you better do these or else you're in trouble*). Christians live under God's law of love. It ought not be hard to obey God if we have a relationship of love and we want to please him (Matthew 11:29-30; 1 John 5:3).

LOVE OTHERS

To love God means to love others as he has loved us (John 13:34; 1 John 4:20-21). Like Jesus laid down his life for us, love is sacrificial (John 15:13). Although sacrificial love may mean giving up our physical life in death if God calls us to that, mostly, loving others means it costs us in time or money to give others our personal care. We are to walk in love (Ephesians 5:1-2), striving to let all we do be done in love (1 Corinthians 16:14). To love means to serve others by doing good and meeting needs. Whom are we called to love? We are called to love fellow believers (1 John 4:10-11), any person in need whom God brings across our path (Luke 10:25-37; Leviticus 19:18; Romans 13:8-10; Galatians 5:13-14), and all people in general, including those who do not love us, even our enemies (Galatians 6:10; Luke 6:27-33). We cannot love God and at the same time hate others and refuse to do good for them. Furthermore, there is no racism among God's people, for he makes people from every tribe, tongue, people, and nation to be his people. All whom God saves are one in Christ Jesus, Jews and Gentiles alike (Revelation 5:9-10; Ephesians 2:14-22). As God loves the world and gives of himself to save it, as his representatives so do we.

Loving others as Jesus did is perhaps the most difficult thing for us to learn. In fact, it is impossible without his help (John 15:4-5). When we walk in the Spirit, we can do it, but not when we are giving in to our old wrongful ways (Galatians 5:16-26). Perhaps you, like myself, have struggled with living out the kind of love Jesus lived and taught. There is something about it that puts our lives at risk. We put ourselves at risk when giving up our own desires for the good of others. In some cases, we risk being physically harmed or put to death when standing for what is right in the midst of a world where wrongdoing and evils surround us. In truth, to be able to love as Jesus loves, one must be prepared to die, both to self-will and to the prospect of physical death. Therefore, the next two ways we love God are vitally important to being able to love as he loves. We must spend time with God whose presence is ever with us, and we must trust God and the hope he gives us that no matter what, we have a future with him (Proverbs 23:17-18; Psalm 71:4-5; 62:5-8).

SPEND TIME WITH HIM

To love God means to spend time with him, talking with him and he with us. Jesus said something in the last book of the Bible about himself and us. He said, "Behold I stand at the door and knock; if anyone hears my voice and opens the door; I will come into him and will dine with him and he with me" (Revelation 3:20). He wants a personal relationship with us. We can carry on conversation with him anywhere and anytime—and I do, but I have too often ignored taking time apart from my busyness just to be with him and to talk and listen. It helps to have a special time and place to meet where we feel unhurried and can be silent before him. Talking is the easy part. We always have things we want to say, and we can be very honest with him. I can tell him anything—what is good, what I like or don't like, and what bad things are going on in my life. Listening to him is where we often flounder. I have learned that he speaks to me in his Word, the Bible. I have also learned how to recognize his voice in my conscience. When I get alone with him and have a Bible, I read it with a prayer that he will tell me things he wants me to know. Good examples of personal communication with God are found in Psalms 16–19. I encourage you to read those chapters, and other psalms, to notice how the psalmist speaks to God and what he hears God saying back to him.

I was under a pastor who preached a five-week series on Colossians chapter 3. He challenged us to read that chapter every day for five weeks. My wife helped me get started by asking if I did it (I needed that). We were to pick out one of the many action verbs in the chapter and put it into practice (there must be at least thirty of them in that chapter). I picked out a word that stood out to me as something God wanted me to work on in my daily life. I looked up that word's meaning in a dictionary, thought about ways I could do it, and asked God to help me. To me, it was a great exercise in spending time with God and listening to the things he was telling me concerning how to live my life in a way that honors him.

TRUST HIM

To love God means to trust him in all circumstances (Proverbs 3:5-6). Jesus says to address God as our heavenly Father (Matthew 6:9). Why can we trust God? We can trust him because he is different from earthly fathers. Some earthly fathers are pretty good and deserve our respect, while others may be very bad and are hard to respect. But none are perfect. God is a perfect Father (Matthew 5:48). The more we see who our heavenly Father is and know what he does for us, the more we will realize he is worthy of our love, respect, and trust. We can trust that he is with us and will never leave or forsakes us (Deuteronomy 31:6). We can trust his promises and the hope he gives us. We can trust that "even though [we] walk through the valley of the shadow of death, [we need] fear no evil," for he is with us (Psalm 23:4).

As we meditate on Scriptures that talk about our Father in heaven, we learn more about what we can expect from him. Our Father considers us to be of great worth to him. We are to trust that he will take care of us, and we are not to be worried about our life (Matthew 6:25-26). Our Father, according to his great mercy, gives us life; he caused us to be born again to a living hope through the resurrection of Jesus (1 Peter 1:3). Our Father has bestowed great love on us by calling us his children (1 John 3:1). Our Father is like a vinedresser who prunes us so that we can have more fruitful lives (John 15:1-2). Our Father disciplines us for our good so that we can have strong and holy character like his (Hebrews 12:5-10). Our

Father is a potter, and we are the clay whom he forms by his own hand into a good and useful vessel (Isaiah 64:8). Our Father is the giver of every good and perfect gift from above (James 1:17). Our Father is merciful and comforts us in all our afflictions (2 Corinthians 1:3-4). Our Father has many other names in the Bible that reveal what he is like. He is a God of peace (Judges 6:24) and a God who provides what we need (Genesis 22:7-8, 14). We are trusting him when we believe who he is and receive what he offers.

CONCLUDING WORDS

To review what it means to love God, we have said that it begins by experiencing his love through his daily kindnesses, repentance, forgiveness, and the gift of his Holy Spirt and new birth to eternal life. Then we respond by loving him, not out of duty but out of gratitude. We love him by putting him above everything else in our lives, worshiping him, fearing him, obeying his commandments, loving others as he has loved us, spending time with him, and trusting him in all circumstances. Will we be able to love him perfectly in these ways? Not always, but we can in those times when we are walking in his Spirit (Galatians 5:16, 22-24).

You may have heard the statement that God's love is unconditional. Certainly it is in the sense that we are continually accepted for who we are, we are loved and forgiven and not judged and condemned for our wrongs, and he never leaves or forsakes those whom he loves (John 10:27-30). We can be secure and feel secure in this. On the other hand, his love is also conditional in the sense that it requires a reciprocal response on our part. Unconditional and conditional love work together. This is true in any loving relationship. For example, the relationship between husbands and wives, if it is truly a loving relationship, cannot work if there is not giving and receiving from both parties. It must work that way because that is how it works in the personhood of God himself. The Father loves the Son, and the Son loves the Father, and we humans are created in his image. Jesus is our best human model for what it means to love God. We can observe how he does it on the pages of Scripture, both Old and New Testaments. And as we practice his love, others can learn it from us.

POSTSCRIPT:
LIVING A SUCCESSFUL CHRISTIAN LIFE

As I age in my life and grow in my walk with Jesus, I continue to learn what is important and needed to live a successful and fruitful Christian life. What I share with you now is something I wish I had begun more consistently many years ago. We Christians often find we are living our Christian life too sporadically. We need more consistency in doing God's will and work daily—actually, not just daily but moment by moment. It is never too late to begin improving our ways to honor the Lord.

If we are to be more successful in living the Christian life, we need to believe what the Bible says about humans. The prophet Jeremiah said, "The heart is more deceitful than all else and is desperately sick; who can understand it?" (Jeremiah 17:9). Jesus said, "For from within, out of the heart of men proceed the evil thoughts [see his list of evil thoughts and actions]. All these evil things proceed from within and defile the man" (Mark 7:21-23). The Apostle Paul said concerning himself, "For I know that nothing good dwells in me, that is, in my flesh; for the willing is present in me, but the doing of the good is not. For the good that I want to do, I do not do, but I practice the very evil that I do not want . . . I find then the principle that evil is present in me, the one who wants to do good" (Romans 7:18-21). Paul's conclusion in Romans 7:24 was, "Wretched man that I am! Who will set me free from the body of this death?" Fortunately for him and for us, there was an answer. "Thanks be to God through Jesus Christ our Lord!" (Romans 7:25).

The Bible is absolutely right in its assessment of humans. All too often we automatically make wrong choices, think wrong thoughts, say wrong things, and react wrongly to various situations that happen throughout each day. Even though wanting to be and do good may be there, we are powerless to achieve it, powerless to overcome our sinful human nature. It seems that the normal default of humans is forgetting how bad off we are in terms of our corruption. We are all far away from the good humans God created in the beginning. Do you and I believe this? I mean, really believe it and acknowledge it?

Humanism is a philosophy that thinks we can be good without God. Obviously they do not believe what the Bible says about human nature. Alcoholics believe it. They say, "We are powerless, and our life is unmanageable." They know that they cannot overcome their addiction without divine help. All humans are addicted to sin, their lives are powerless and unmanageable, and sin cannot be overcome without divine help. Only a good, gracious, and powerful God can save us. The Christian God gives us what we need to help us overcome our prideful and self-centered nature.

We all need a God who can do two things. First, God must have a way to get us to see how blind and corrupt and deceived we are so that we become willing to seek change. Second, our God must have the power to recreate us into his image of goodness. Humans in this world can never be good as God is good. They will forever fail. There is only one hope to be saved from ourselves, from our human fallenness, from the evils of this world, and from death. We must have our eyes opened to the truth and submit to the only God who can save us. When we do submit to God and receive from God everything we need for a life of godliness, we must take into account the corrupted nature within us and learn to surrender moment by moment to walking in his ways. He tells us that if we walk by his Spirit, we will not carry out the desires of the flesh (Galatians 5:16).

Like the alcoholic twelve steps for recovery, which are Bible based, we must be continually aware that we are powerless to change ourselves. These steps have helped many alcoholics and others with other kinds of addictive behaviors to overcome and live free from the destruction of the addiction in their lives. It is not that they learn step one, master it, and move on to step two, master it, and move on to step three, and so forth. It doesn't work that way. For them to be successful, they must learn to practice these twelve steps each day. The more they practice them, the more they become second nature and part of a new lifestyle. When we practice the awareness that we are powerless to change ourselves, and when we continually surrender to Christ and the power of his Spirit, we are changed. Without him, we can do nothing (John 15:5).

If we are not prepared for whatever is coming by walking in the Holy Spirit, our weakness is ready to take over at any given time and in any situation throughout the day. I am becoming more convinced that I need to rely on God moment by moment. Jesus was tempted by the devil, not just during his forty days in the wilderness but at future opportune times as well (Luke 4:1-15). Opportune times are times of weakness, thoughtlessness, and unawareness. In Luke's temptation account, we also see that when Jesus left the wilderness to do his daily ministry, he went in the power of the Holy Spirit. The devil likes to attack us in areas of our weakness. Walking in the Spirit will enable us to recognize his attack and be ready to resist him so that he flees.

Regarding a moment-by-moment approach to living by the Spirit, I came across something in my reading of the Old Testament that I never thought applied to me. In Exodus 30:1-10, God is instructing Moses to make an altar for burning incense. Aaron, God's high priest, was to burn fragrant incense on it, not just at special times but every morning. It was to be a perpetual incense before the Lord. This brought to mind a Scripture found in 2 Corinthians 2:14-15, which tells us that as Christians, God "manifests through us the sweet aroma of the knowledge of him in every place. For we are the fragrance of Christ to God among those who are being saved and among those who are perishing." This aroma, like on the altar of incense, is to be a daily perpetual thing unto the Lord. This *fragrance of Christ* verse is located in a context that says, "Thanks be to God, who always leads us in triumph in Christ." As we walk in the Spirit, moment by moment, we are the sweet-smelling fragrance of Christ to God among those around us.

So how do we walk by the Holy Spirit on a moment-by-moment basis? How can we continually be filled with the Holy Spirit as implied in Ephesians 5:18? This is not something easy, nor something totally in our control, for God must also be allowed to be in control. Our world tells us in some of its messages to *take control of your life*, but the truth is that we don't know enough, nor are we strong enough, to completely do that. That's why it is good to know that we have a good God who loves us and who is in control of our well-being when we are not. Walking by the Spirit will enable us to live a Christ-centered life more consistently.

WHAT DOES IT MEAN TO WALK BY THE SPIRIT?

- To walk by the Spirit, we must believe the Spirit of God is always with us and is living in us.

- To walk by the Spirit, we must believe the Holy Spirit guides us in the ways of God.

- To walk by the Spirit, we must understand how the Spirit communicates and works to guide us.

- To walk by the Spirit, we must be guided. The Bible tells us at least two ways he guides us: the Spirit speaks to us using clear words, and the Spirit works out circumstances in our lives to help point us in the direction to go.

- To walk by the Spirit, we must put ourselves in a position to hear his voice and heed his workings.

  » One way we position ourselves to hear his voice is to become as knowledgeable as possible with the book the Spirit wrote, which we call the Bible. The Spirit can then remind us of his words when we need them for various situations. Being in God's Scriptures is certainly a great way to be continually reminded of God's will and ways to live. Peter recorded the word of the Lord to provide reminders of God's truths so readers could remember to practice their faith and recall the hope that sustains them in difficult times (2 Peter 1:12-15).

  » Another way to be in position to hear his voice is through continually and often being in person-to-person communication with him. This gives the Spirit the opportunity to speak his message directly into our minds, Mind to mind, Spirit to spirit. Constant prayer (talking with God) keeps our heart and mind set on the Lord and the things he cares about, not just what concerns me but also others.

» We can be in position to recognize the Spirit's workings in our hearts and through life's circumstances by telling the Lord what we need and asking him to help us. Admittedly, we often do not see the Spirit's workings until after something happens. Then we recognize his answers to our needs and his workings in our life, and we give thanks to him. Sometimes we are surprised by his providential workings, especially when we had not asked for anything, he just did it because he cares.

» To be in position to hear God speak and see him work, we must keep ourselves out of the way. We do this by being aware of our sin and overcoming it with the help of the Lord so that we stay clean and open to God's voice and ways (1 John 3:4-10). We invite the Holy Spirit to convict us of wrongs in our lives whenever he sees fit. For example, Peter had to be corrected by the Lord when he objected to something Jesus said. Jesus rebuked Peter and said, "Get behind me Satan; for you are not setting your mind on God's interests, but man's" (Mark 8:33).

» We stay in position for God to help and lead us by remaining positive and hopeful, knowing that when things go wrong, all will be OK. We can remain positive by knowing the hope God has given us and by relying on the truth that God is with us and will fulfill for us all that he has promised.

» I choose to live by Proverbs 3:5-6: "Trust in the Lord with all your heart, lean not on your own understanding, in all your ways acknowledge him, and he will direct your path."

• To walk by the Spirit, we can develop a moment-by-moment spiritual mindset that keeps us hearing and heeding him.

(Please note: the following is what I have deemed I need for my life. You are free to decide how you want or need God to work in your life. If anything I have shared in this postscript helps you, praise God, and run with it.)

WHAT WALKING BY THE SPIRIT FOR ME DOES NOT MEAN

- It does not mean asking him to make all my choices for me of what I am to do every day. My life continues as it normally does. God gives me freedom to choose what I do, and I take responsibility for my choices and what I plan each day.

- It does not mean asking him to bless all my plans and expecting him to make everything to turn out all right. Some things I choose may be wrong choices that need to be corrected. I give the Spirit permission to change anything in my life that he sees needs changing. I am free to make mistakes and learn from them.

- It does not mean things will always run smoothly. There are lots of areas of life we cannot control. Bad things can happen, and God may allow them for good reasons. But I need God to help me through the bad times with appropriate responses on my part.

WHAT WALKING BY THE SPIRIT FOR ME DOES MEAN

It means having a goal and a plan to meet that goal.

My goal:

- To obey the Scriptures that say, "Keep seeking the things above, where Christ is" (Colossians 3:1); "be filled with the Spirit" (Ephesians 5:18); "be transformed by the renewing of your mind" (Romans 12:2); "walk by the Spirit, and you will not carry out the desire of the flesh" (Galatians 5:16); and "resist the devil and he will flee from you" (James 4:7).

- To overcome the Apostle Paul's problem, "I am not practicing what I would like to do, but I am doing the very thing I hate" (Romans 7:15). For example, when I get irritated with someone, often I will not practice God's love but will do what I don't want, which is to become angry and say or do the wrong thing. I want to be godly and wise in my responses to what is going on in and around me.

- To realize that I am crucified with Christ and the life I live, I live by faith in the Son of God who loved me and gave his life for me (Galatians 2:20).

- To address the Father and/or the Son in my requests and rely on the power of the Holy Spirit to be my helper, doing God's work in me and through me. The Father sent the Son to be our Savior. The Savior said to address the Father in our communications. Jesus also gives us the Holy Spirit to be our Comforter and Helper and to empower us to do God's will. Jesus is Lord and lives in us by the Holy Spirit, and the Spirit glorifies the Son. In my walking by the Spirit, I want the Holy Spirit to help me glorify God in all I think, say, or do. I want to surrender or submit to the power of the Holy Spirit moment by moment.

My goal is to practice cooperating with God in working out my salvation, realizing God is at work in me, "Both to will and to work for his good pleasure" (Philippians 2:12-13). The result will be to see the fruit of the Spirit in my life—love, joy, peace . . . (Galatians 5:22-23).

My plan to meet the goal:

- I will seek to address God the Father and/or the Lord Jesus Christ and ask to be filled with the Holy Spirit for each and every activity or event I am about to enter into throughout the day. I will ask for what I need in order to honor him and his purposes and to be his love to others. If I sense the need for his help in the midst of an activity or event, I will use a short prayer to ask his help. God knows what I desire and need. "Lord, help me," will suffice as a quick prayer in time of need.

177

- My prayer will be, "Lord, fill me with your Spirit as I
  _____" (name the coming event or activity). "I need
  you to _____" (tell him your need or desire).

- When I see how God helped me, I will give praise and
  thanks to him. If opportunity comes, I will humbly give
  him credit and tell others what he has done.

A STUDY GUIDE FOR INDIVIDUALS OR GROUPS

FOR THE LEADER

The following format provides suggestions if you need ideas for leading group discussion. The same format can be used for the preface and each chapter. Some chapters in this book may have questions for study and discussion within the chapter.

Be prepared by reading the material and Bible verses and personally answering some of the discussion and application questions. This helps you add personal input into the discussion.

Choose what questions to ask the group. You may have some of your own.

As followers of Jesus, our relationships need to become deeper than just information sharing. A key purpose of the group is to get to know one another, build deeper friendships, share life stories, and develop loving support by meeting one another's needs. Allow discussion to take its natural course—it is OK to deviate from the script. Decide when to get back on task.

DISCUSSION THAT CAN APPLY TO EACH CHAPTER

1. Consider the title of the chapter. Why would you be interested, or not, in the topic?

2. Read the opening paragraph(s) of the chapter. What thoughts or experiences come to mind?

3. Include the Scripture references when reading the paragraphs. Stop and discuss any paragraph you or the group want(s) to explore further.

   » What is your response to what was just read?

   » What point do you think is being made?

   » How does the verse, or verses, support or not support the point being made?

> » Where do you agree or disagree?

> » Do you have anything to add to the topic being discussed that could benefit you or your group?

> » Are there questions that come to mind?

> » Can you share any personal stories that came to mind from the paragraph or Scriptures?

> » What have you heard others you know, or various media in the world, say about this subject?

4. When discussing Bible passages, the following are appropriate questions:

> » What does this text say?

> » What does this word (any word in the text) mean?

> » Who is speaking, and why do they say what they say? (Note the context surrounding the verse.)

> » What is God asking us to be or do?

> » What would be the results if we obeyed what it said?

> » Do you have any questions about the passage?

5. Application questions—Choose whatever ones work for you or your group:

> » What did you learn?

> » How does this information benefit your life? What would happen if you ignored it?

> » What would you like to do with this information?

> » If you want to put this into practice in your life, how can others help you?

> » Is there any way you can use this information to benefit family or friends?

> » How or when would be a right time to pass on some of these concepts to my kids?

> » Is anyone struggling with anything involving this topic? (Be sensitive to each other's needs.)

OTHER BOOKS BY JAY R. ASHBAUCHER

THE POWER OF LIFE-GIVING HOPE IN TROUBLESOME TIMES

Book 1 in the "Upload Your Faith" series

Troublesome times are increasing. Scanning the news and seeing what is happening around the world leaves many with anxieties, fears, and depression. Moral decline, increasing violence, terrorism, and threats of war are everywhere. Americans fear things like a divided country, not having enough money, identity theft, natural disasters, mass shootings, and walking alone at night. Employers complain of difficulty finding reliable workers, and experienced school teachers say it's harder to teach. For Christians, increased persecution is at hand. What's the world coming to? is a common thought in people's minds. Good news! There is hope! This book offers hope and mentions three different kinds. The kind of hope you have makes a difference in the kind of life you live. You can experience a hope that brings joy and peace of mind in the midst of adversity. This book is about knowing the Creator of hope and how this Creator would have us live in times like these. It's about finding life-giving hope that fulfills its promises for a trouble-free world.

FAITH

Book 2 in the "Upload Your Faith" series

Faith always has an object. What you and I believe in is what we rely on to give us what we need and want. There are two important questions to consider:

1. Is what or whom we believe in capable of giving us what we need and want?

2. Is what we think we need and want the same as what we truly need?

This book defines faith, answers questions about faith, shows how and why faith works, helps us identify weaknesses and strengths of our faith, challenges us to consider God as the ultimate source of faith, and gives insights on how faith enables us to overcome problems we face. Examples include how faith helps one overcome addictions and how faith helps one establish a positive self-identity. The goal of this book is to help readers grow in understanding and practicing genuine faith, thus becoming the person God created us to be.

OUT OF DARKNESS INTO THE LIGHT: LEARNING TO SEE LIFE FROM GOD'S POINT OF VIEW

Based on Jesus' words that He is *the Light of the world*, this book will help believers better understand their faith and live a richer and more satisfying life. It will assist those who have not yet trusted Jesus to understand what the Christian Way is about so they can come to a more intelligent decision on whether to follow Jesus, or not. The book contains 26 chapters on various subjects to help believers explore and make sense out of everyday questions or issues they may encounter, experience the energy of new life in Christ, and gain hope that sustains them through life's difficulties. To discover Jesus' love, wisdom, and peace is the ultimate aim of the book, but requires that we come out of darkness and into the light.

BUILDING A LIFE WITH GOD: *A Study for Individuals and Groups*

This book uses the metaphor of building a house (along with other metaphors) to describe what it is like to build a life with God. We live in a world of growing instability and problems. People need a house that offers them safety and well-being. Everyone needs a safe place to live, a place that lasts. Many think a life with God is all going to heaven when we die. God's plan is much bigger than that.

BUILDING A LIFE WITH GOD: *Workbook*

This booklet is a personal or group study that can be used alone or as a companion to the *Building a Life With God* book. It provides six studies in the format of questions. Individuals can discover what the Bible says and can write their answers in the book.

Books are available at your favorite outlets, including InnovoPublishing.com, Christianbook.com, Barnes and Noble, Amazon.com, Books-A-Million.com, AbeBooks.com, and other fine resellers.

AUTHOR'S WEBSITE: JAY-ASHBAUCHER.COM

www.ingramcontent.com/pod-product-compliance
Lightning Source LLC
LaVergne TN
LVHW021447080426
835509LV00018B/2189